REGENCY
STYLE

Steven Parissien

REGENCY STYLE

THE PRESERVATION PRESS
NATIONAL TRUST FOR HISTORIC PRESERVATION

The Preservation Press
National Trust for Historic Preservation
1785 Massachusetts Avenue, N.W.
Washington, D.C. 20036

The National Trust for Historic Preservation in the United States is the only national private nonprofit
organization chartered by Congress to encourage public participation in the preservation of sites,
buildings and objects significant in American history and culture. Support is provided by membership
dues, endowment funds, contributions and grants from federal agencies, including the U.S. Department
of the Interior, under provisions of the National Historic Preservation Act of 1966. The opinions
expressed in this publication do not necessarily reflect the views or policies of the Interior Department.
For information about membership, write to the Trust at the above address.

Library of Congress Cataloging-in-Publication Data

Parissien, Steven.
 Regency style/Steven Parissien.
   p.   cm.
 Includes bibliographical references (p.   ) and index.
 ISBN 0-89133-172-7
 1. Decoration and ornament—Great Britain—Regency style.
 2. Architecture. Regency—Great Britain. 3. Furniture, Regency
 —Great Britain. I. Title.
NK928.P33 1992
728',0941'09034—dc20

Originally published in Great Britain by Phaidon Press Limited

Printed and bound in Singapore 1992

Designed by Pocknell and Green

ACKNOWLEDGEMENTS

I would like to thank all those who have helped in the production of this book, most notably
Frances Collard and Clive Wainwright of the Victoria and Albert Museum; Adam White of
Temple Newsam House; Cynthia Jones, Jean Monro, Marie Frank and Caroline Rimell for their
suggestions regarding American sources; the staff of *Traditional Homes* magazine and of the R.I.B.A.
Drawings Collection for their help and generous loan of photographs. Above all, I would particularly
like to thank Kit Wedd for her painstaking proofreading and invaluable suggestions.

Frontispiece
*Henry Holland's Hall at Carlton House, London, begun in 1785 for Prince George.
Drawn and engraved by A. C. Pugin and Thomas Rowlandson in 1809 – twelve years before its
demolition. This view shows some of the Ionic columns and pilasters executed in highly fashionable
yellow brocatello marble.*

The Green Closet at Frogmore, Berkshire, from Pyne's Royal Residences. *The house was fitted out for the Regent's mother, Queen Charlotte, after 1803. This is a splendid example of the Regency taste for chinoiserie, with its 'Chinese' wallpaper and japanned furniture. Note the 'cloud' ceiling – a fashion very much in evidence in the early years of the nineteenth century, yet one which had largely fallen out of favour by 1830. This marvellous house is now open to the public.*

The Regency was a marvellous period for the visual arts. It was a time in architecture when Palladian grandeur was fused with Neo-Classical academicism and with the vivid visions of gifted designers such as Soane and Hope. Colours were more exotic and vibrant than they had been for centuries; the ubiquitous brilliant white paint and ruthlessly stripped woodwork of many of today's 'historic' interiors were certainly not to Regency taste. It was also a period which witnessed the introduction of many familiar labour-saving devices and products, which constitute such a fascinating bridge between Georgian taste and modern comfort.

The Regency is also, however, a style which has been much abused by modern manufacturers and supposedly expert commentators. There are many books on the market telling you how to exploit historical 'features', which bandy about words such as 'tone' and 'look' with carefree abandon. This is not one of them. It does not comprise bogus historic interiors featuring the vaguely historical ideas of one particular designer, nor the reproduction products from a few suppliers. It seeks to tell you what actually happened during the period, and to explain how architectural and decorative patterns and solutions evolved. If you are keen to restore or redecorate your own home, you can use this information as you yourself see fit – relying principally on your *own* judgement, not just on the opinions of so-called experts.

If you are seeking to refurbish your home, this book does not aim to convince you that whatever was done in the Regency period should be attempted today. To recapture the exact conditions of 1790 or 1840 would be quite impossible, and the results would always smack of tokenism; after all, to go the whole hog, you may as well eliminate education, forget to wash, not bother with modern medicine, avoid the private car and public transport. I do not suggest that you take your kitchen or your bathroom back to Regency standards. The whole approach to a historic house, of whatever period, must always be one of sensible compromise, of pragmatism as well as enthusiasm. What this book does preach is the virtue of sensitivity, and the benefits to be reaped from avoiding the precious pretentiousness that is such a feature of many of today's 'period' interiors.

Over-dramatization of this sort often derives from taking inappropriately grand examples as models for your own modest home. These may have been culled from the great houses of Britain, many of which are open to the public; while these can be useful sources, they do have their limitations. We cannot all live in Sezincote or Shugborough – nor, I think, would we all want to. *Regency Style* does not include an analysis of the great houses and the great architects of Regency Britain; this area has already been admirably and expertly covered by authors such as Dr David Watkin. Instead the book concentrates principally on the *average* house.

This is not, however, a book only for would-be restorers or redecorators; it is for anyone who is at all interested in this most fascinating of eras. *Regency Style* is first and foremost a book to dip into. If you wish to learn more about a particular subject, there is a wealth of Further Reading detailed at the end. There is also a section on reliable professional bodies who can provide you with information and with names of suppliers.

Steven Parissien
January 1992

NOT A FATTER FISH THAN HE
FLOUNDERS ROUND THE POLAR SEA . . .
BY HIS BULK AND BY HIS SIZE
BY HIS OILY QUALITIES,
THIS (OR ELSE MY EYESIGHT FAILS)
THIS SHOULD BE THE PRINCE OF WHALES.

(CHARLES LAMB)

The phrase 'Regency style' is one redolent of luxury and pomp, dripping with images of opulence and innate good taste, with the fabulously primped figure of the Prince Regent himself at its epicentre. It characterizes an age marvellously rich in political, industrial, and artistic triumphs. 'Regency Britain' is the Britain of Trafalgar and Waterloo; of Watt and Stephenson; of Jane Austen and Sir Walter Scott; of Shelley and Wordsworth; of Turner and Nash. More tragic heroes bestride this short period than the rest of the eighteenth century put together: Keats perishing miserably in Rome; Nelson breathing his last on the deck of the *Victory*; Byron expiring heroically in revolutionary Greece. The era is not short on comic vignettes, either: the Prince of Wales, horribly drunk at a party for the Whig politician Charles James Fox, falling flat on his face in the middle of the ballroom and being violently sick; the playwright and Whig leader Richard Sheridan staggering drunk and insensible into the House of Commons; William IV's memorable toast after an incoherent speech to diplomats at St James's Palace: 'To eyes that kill, the thighs that rouse, and bums which dance – honi soit qui mal y pense'.

Yet though the phrase is frequently used, not many are entirely clear exactly what or when the 'Regency period' was. The term 'Regency' is one of the most shamelessly abused labels in the contemporary worlds of marketing and design. The result is that the word 'Regency' often becomes quite meaningless, devoid of any historical accuracy or stylistic worth. The 'Regency period' was not, it must be emphasized, merely a time of glittering luxury and over-indulgence. What the purveyors of sham-Regency products seem to forget is that the Regency was also a time of great social unrest and injustice. Jane Austen's exquisite novels, for example, fail to explain that it was an age in which violence constantly threatened to explode.

From 1789 onwards agitation for Parliamentary and social reform in Britain, inspired by events across the Channel, was suppressed only by recourse to savage penal legislation, such as the notorious Seditious Meetings and Treasonable Practices Acts of 1792. The Regency was the age of the

A view of Keats's House, in Hampstead, London. A typical urban home of the early nineteenth century.

Brighton Pavilion, Sussex, from the east.

Peterloo Massacre – the shooting of peaceful protesters by the local militia in Manchester in 1819; of the hated Corn Laws – legislation explicitly designed to protect the landowners' profits at the expense of the rest of the country. It was a time when the death penalty was prescribed for petty theft, for forgery, and for poaching – all crimes which threatened private property. Slavery was abolished in 1807; yet in 1793 almost a quarter of the workforce of the philanthropic industrialist Robert Owen was under nine years old.

During the early 1830s revolution was widely anticipated in Britain, particularly during the frustration of repeated attempts at Parliamentary reform before 1832 and after William IV's abrupt dismissal of Lord Grey's reforming Whig government in 1834. In 1831, with serious rioting in Bristol and rural violence all over southern England, the leading liberal Whig, Lord Macaulay, advocated the passing of the new Parliamentary Reform Bill as the only means by which the revolutions which had recently erupted in France and Belgium could be avoided in Britain. The sophisticated pomp and pageantry of the Prince Regent's Brighton Pavilion, it must be remembered, was devised only a year or two after the last Jacobites' heads had been taken down from the spikes on London's Temple Bar and the last woman had been burned at the stake for murdering her husband. It was a time when the mob was still very much a force to be reckoned with. In 1816 – a year after Waterloo and the year in which Jane Austen's *Mansfield Park* was published – the Regent himself was shot at as his carriage attempted to force a passage through the London mobs.

There are also many misconceptions as to the actual extent of the 'Regency period'. In strictly political terms, the Regency was surprisingly short. George III's last and most serious illness – not, we now guess, simple insanity but probably the debilitating blood disorder porphyria – commenced on 25 October 1810, and on 6 February 1811 the Prince of Wales took the oaths of office as Regent. (The subsequent celebration cost a massive £120,000; Shelley predicted that this would not be 'the last bauble which the nation must buy to amuse this overgrown bantling of Regency'.) Nine years later, on 29 January 1820, the blind, tormented and deranged old king died, and the Regent was proclaimed King George IV. In artistic terms, however, the 'Regency period' extends further than the political parameters of the Regency itself, being generally taken to encompass the last years of the eighteenth century and the reigns of both George IV (1820–30) and William IV (1830–7) – i.e. the last third of the Georgian period, together with what historian Dr Tim Mowl has recently termed the 'Williamane'.

There is, of course, a great danger in defining this or any other stylistic era too precisely. Artistic or architectural periods were not suddenly decreed and did not take immediate effect. Stylistic movements evolved and adapted, and what was being introduced in London or Edinburgh was not necessarily reflected in what was being designed in Penzance, Leeds, or Inverness. It is perhaps, then, best to avoid a rigid chronological definition, in which the first application of 'Regency Style' can be definitively traced to 1780, 1783, 1790, or some other particular point, or indeed said to have ceased abruptly at such necessarily arbitrary dates as 1820, 1830, 1837, or 1840. A house built in 1836, which the architectural historian – or, indeed, the property dealer – may describe as 'Regency' or 'William IV', may very well be identical to a so-called 'Victorian' house of 1837, or for that matter to a 'Georgian' house built in 1787.

Too precise a use of dates is therefore rather misleading. One particular year, though, does seem to serve as a useful portent of the Regency era: 1783 was first and foremost the year in which the Prince of Wales came into his majority and also the year in which he first visited the then little-regarded Sussex fishing village of Brighthelmstone – soon to be reincarnated as the fashionable, scandalous seaside resort of Brighton. It was also the year of the Treaty of Paris, which ended the American War of Independence. While formally severing these colonies from the Motherland, the treaty indirectly encouraged Britain to look eastwards and southwards for both her imperial and her artistic inspiration, setting the foundations for Victoria's Empire and, in the more domestic world of interior design, for the multiplicity of exotic styles which characterized the 1820s and 1830s. It was in 1783, too, that the last ostensibly Whig government for almost half a century held office: following his appointment as Prime Minister by George III at the ludicrously early age of twenty-four, William Pitt began to mould Britain into what was by 1794 virtually a one-party state, a process continued after 1812 by the Earl of Liverpool and his 'liberal' Tory governments. It was also in 1783 that the engineer James Watt invented the term 'horse power' to measure the output of his new steam engines, a useful symbol for the rapid growth of the industrial revolution and for the vast transformation of British society – including, of course, British homes – which it effected. Public executions, at the most notorious spot in Britain, Tyburn, ceased in 1783, and the area was soon redeveloped in a far more genteel and respectable guise, now known as Marble Arch. Most significantly in terms of style and taste, in 1783 the architect Henry Holland began work remodelling the Prince of Wales's Carlton House in London, inaugurating a period of more formal Neo-Classical design.

All of these threads perceptible in the events of 1783 – the birth of domestic Neo-Classicism and of the stylistic influence of the Prince, the rapid progress of the industrial revolution, the growing self-confidence and self-awareness of the British nation – can be amalgamated to form a very rough-and-ready definition of what 'Regency style' really signifies. In the arts, the influence of the Prince of Wales, of political developments, of industrial advances, and of the antique served to produce what was undoubtedly a very eclectic style, yet at the same time one that was quintessentially, self-consciously British, in a way no architectural or decorative style had ever been before. The uniqueness of this Britishness was recognized as early as the 1890s, when Liberty's store pioneered a revival in distinctive Regency fabrics; the sale of Thomas Hope's house at Deepdene,

A doorway from Homewood in Baltimore, Maryland. The pale green joinery and bright yellow walls are typical of the period, the house having been remodelled in 1801.

Surrey, in 1917 in turn sparked off a full-blooded Regency Revival during the interwar years which encompassed every element of interior decoration, from armchairs to wallpaper.

'Regency' was also a unique style which could be exported wholesale to the continent and, particularly, to the United States, where the English Regency style had a substantial influence on American design at the time of the Federal and 'Empire' eras of architecture and decoration. Thomas Sheraton's pattern-books sold particularly well in the new Republic; indeed, it is from the United States, not from Britain, that valuable reprints of the works of Sheraton, Hope, Smith, and others have come in recent years. Homewood in Baltimore, refurbished after 1801, is an excellent example of an American home decorated entirely in the new, highly fashionable English Regency manner, using imported English furniture where possible. Benjamin Henry Latrobe, who emigrated to America from Britain in the 1790s and who was subsequently responsible for some of the East Coast's most notable public buildings, serves as a useful symbol of the importation of the latest English styles and conventions into the country. And even Thomas Jefferson, America's third president and one of the Republic's most influential architects, was himself profoundly influenced by contemporary British design. In 1786 Jefferson visited Britain and, with the War of Independence barely over, predictably announced that he was less than impressed with British houses. 'Their architecture is in the most wretched style I ever saw', he declared ('not meaning to except America', he carefully added, 'where it is bad, or even Virginia, where it is worse than in any other part of America.') Yet his architecture – even of his own home, Monticello – remained heavily influenced, not by the French models he so readily quoted but by English styles. And in general both American architecture and American interior decoration during the first decades of the nineteenth century – despite the frequent borrowing of the French term 'Empire' – owed far more to the emerging Regency style than to the forms and manufactures of Napoleonic and Restoration France.

Before looking at the individual, constituent parts of the Regency house in an attempt to dissect the practical realization of Regency style, it may be helpful quickly to examine the style's influences and contexts in a little more detail. This must naturally begin with the effect of Neo-Classicism, a creed whose precepts pervaded every aspect of Regency design. The ancient world, and in particular classical Greece, had been dramatically rediscovered by the British during the 1760s, an enthusiasm largely prompted by published works such as Stuart and Revett's magisterial *The Antiquities of Athens* of 1762. Figures such as Robert Adam, Josiah Wedgwood, and (abandoning his earlier predilection for the 'Gothick') Thomas Chippendale adapted antique Roman and Greek motifs for use on every conceivable object or surface. Before Adam's death in 1792, however, Henry Holland had introduced an austere and academic reaction against Adam's frivolous, light and rather superficial interpretation of ancient forms. Holland's designs were still elegant and restrained, but they expressed more openly their debt to the archaeological discoveries of Greece, Rome, and Egypt, as well as to the heavier 'Directoire' and 'Empire' styles of contemporary France. The Prince's Carlton House emphasized this new direction, effectively launching what we may call Regency style. In 1785, two years after Holland's French craftsmen had started work there, Horace Walpole perceptively noted 'How sick one shall be, after this chaste place, of Mr Adam's gingerbread and sippets of embroidery'.

How the Regent liked to be seen: Thomas Lawrence's dramatic portrait of c.1814. Unsurprisingly, Lawrence was knighted in 1815.

Holland's taste was popularized in the pattern-books of Charles Heathcote Tatham – whom Holland had sent abroad to copy Greek and Roman designs first-hand – and by Thomas Hope, whose widely publicized designs for architecture and furniture were central to the development of the Regency style. (Hope's *Household Furniture and Interior Decoration* of 1807 reached a comparatively limited audience, but many of his designs were incorporated in Rudolph Ackermann's hugely popular periodical, *The Repository of the Arts*, recently reprinted in digest form.) Hope travelled extensively in the Mediterranean, yet while he made great use of the discoveries at Pompeii and Herculaneum, his works generally betray a more chaste and austere Grecian bias when compared with the more ostentatious, Roman-based ornament used frequently by the French designers of the Empire and the Bourbon Restoration. In 1807 Sydney Smith complained of Hope's influence that, 'having banished the heathen gods' from the literary arts, 'we are to habitually introduce them into our eating rooms, nurseries, and stair-cases'. In place of Rococo exuberance and Adam frippery, Hope's straight lines, restrained ornament, and academic references now prevailed.

Regency style, however, derived from more than just the application of forms and motifs from the ancient world. More than at any other time in Britain's history, politics and particularly personalities affected design to a considerable extent. The most important individual influence was of course the Prince Regent, George IV, himself. His patronage of the arts – which contrasted so dramatically with the homespun, domesticated idylls of his father – was vital to the propagation of the Regency style. Holland's pioneering work at Carlton House has already been noted; in 1806 Holland's calm interiors were themselves remodelled in a riot of crimson and gold by a prince ever anxious to promote, not to lag behind, innovation in interior design. Prince George was indeed the most active royal patron of the arts since Charles I – perhaps a rather apt parallel in more ways than one, given the public's reception of both figures. He was a keen devotee of the novels of Sir Walter Scott and Jane Austen, who dedicated *Mansfield Park* to the Regent in 1816. He was the enthusiastic patron of the artists Wilkie and Lawrence, of the sculptors Canova and Chantrey, and he supported the purchase of the Elgin Marbles. Perhaps his most celebrated artistic association was with the architect John Nash. Nash, whose wife was widely reported to be a past mistress of the Prince's, was loaded with royal commissions: the rebuilding of Buckingham Palace, the remodelling of

Carlton House Terrace, The Mall, London. Built by Nash in 1827–33 as the southern termination of his grand, stucco-clad scheme for a new London for George IV.

Brighton Pavilion, the construction of numerous other royal residences and, most famously, the realization of the vast Regent's Park development. The resultant royal expenditure was predictably massive: even Nash's relatively modest Royal Lodge in Windsor Great Park, for example, had cost £52,000 – an enormous sum then – by 1814, when it was still far from finished; unsurprisingly, it was demolished without ceremony after George IV's death in 1830. Nash's work was far from universally admired by contemporaries: much of the work at Buckingham Palace was structurally unsound and was replaced twenty years later, while the diarist Maria Edgeworth found nothing to praise in the tremendous terraces of Regent's Park, with their 'horrid useless domes and pediments crowded with mock sculpture figures'.

Prince George as satirized by the cartoonist James Gillray. Compare this popular view of the Prince with Lawrence's highly flattering and heroic portrait on page 14.

The Dining Room at Brighton Pavilion. Built for the Prince of Wales by Henry Holland in 1786–7, it was remodelled after 1815 by John Nash in a fantastic Indo-Chinese style.

Yet, for the most part, George IV's keen interest in architecture and decoration served as a catalyst for the corresponding enthusiasm of his subjects. Immediately the remodelled Carlton House was opened to the public in 1811, 30,000 visitors flocked in a single day to see its legendary interiors. In the same year Ackermann introduced the Regent's badge as Prince of Wales – a plume of feathers – into the furniture designs featured in his *Repository*, and by 1812 it was reported that the plume was now a 'prevailing ornament' in domestic interiors. The Prince also popularized the trend from chinoiserie – a fashion which was decidedly less popular following the Emperor of China's brusque rebuff to Lord McCartney's trading mission in 1794 – to the 'Indian' style, pioneered at Cockerell's Sezincote yet popularly enshrined in Nash's new Pavilion at Brighton. George's grotesquely over-romanticized and over-elaborate tour to Scotland in 1823 – a pageant largely organized by Sir Walter Scott – initiated the fashion for all things tartan and bogus-Scots, later taken up with relish by Queen Victoria and which persists to this day.

The influence of the Prince Regent's artistic patronage can be most clearly seen at Brighton. George III's quiet seaside haven of Weymouth was a place where, in the words of the writer John Byng, 'the Irish beau, the gouty peer, and the genteel shopkeeper blend in folly and fine breeding'. Prince George, however, tended to concur with his sister Mary's verdict on Weymouth, that there was nowhere 'more dull and stupid' in Britain. Thus, he acquired a house for himself in Brighton in 1785 (and for his mistress Mrs Fitzherbert in 1786), and by the time he took his oath as Regent, in 1811, he had transformed Brighton into a centre of fashion and taste. To show their gratitude the new burghers of Brighton erected a statue of their benefactor in front of the grand Royal Crescent of 1798–1807; unfortunately, but somewhat aptly, the statue was quickly eroded by the salt winds, and it was not long before one of the Regent's arms had fallen off.

While the person of the Regent was central to the dissemination of Regency fashions, the Prince himself was, with supreme irony, possibly the most universally loathed monarch since Richard II. He had not inspired much public affection even in his earlier years, spending money like water and secretly marrying his Catholic mistress, Mrs Fitzherbert. By the time he

A gilded door from Lancaster House, London.

assumed the Regency – his personal debts standing at a vast £552,000 – he was generally regarded as a dissolute liability. The *Examiner* castigated the new Regent as 'a libertine over head and ears in debt and disgrace, a despiser of romantic ties, the companion of gamblers . . . a man who has just closed half a century without one single claim on the gratitude of his country or the respect of posterity'. To Shelley he was the 'crowned coward and villain' who merely served to supply 'the Augean stable . . . with filth which no second Hercules could cleanse'. Even the celebrated victories of the Allies over Napoleon in 1812–15 failed to improve the Regent's abysmally low standing with his subjects. Nevertheless, the Regency style survived the calumnies heaped upon the head of its greatest advocate; it was strong enough, too, to survive the more typically Hanoverian philistine indifference exhibited by his brother and heir, William IV.

Understanding the role of the Prince Regent is clearly vital to any appreciation of Regency style. So, too, is a grasp of the political context of the period. The wars against France – Revolutionary and Napoleonic – dominated the first half of this era and naturally had a great bearing on all activities, both political and artistic. The Royal Navy's two great victories, the Battles of the Nile (1798) and Trafalgar (1805), seized the public imagination in particular. The anniversary of Nelson's victory of the Nile was widely celebrated well into the 1820s and, coinciding as it did with Tatham and Hope's academic interests in ancient Egypt, spawned a rash of 'Egyptian' motifs – especially sphinxes and crocodiles – adorning almost every decorative item in the house. The furniture-maker Thomas Sheraton incorporated numerous Egyptian forms into the furniture designs of his *Encyclopaedia* of 1804–6; nor was the popularity of the Egyptian taste abated by Ackermann's patrician dismissal of this 'barbarous Egyptian style' in 1809.

Trafalgar, too, prompted a swift response from the architectural and decorative worlds: the classic, sabre-legged chair of the period rapidly became known as the Trafalgar chair; newly fashionable 'Trafalgar balconies' appeared in profusion; Ackermann reproduced elements of his catafalque for Nelson in a variety of more mundane household objects; while shortly before he died in 1806, Sheraton was busily engaged in producing a series of designs for 'Nelson's chairs', with ropes, anchors, dolphins, and other appropriately nautical paraphernalia.

Napoleon's epic retreat from Russia in 1812 prompted a wave of Russian eagles incorporated into furniture and silver designs. 'The eagle of Russia surmounts the whole', explained Ackermann in his notes to a design of 1814, 'in allusion both to the superiority she has obtained in arms and in just compliment to her magnanimous forbearance and her noble and respectful conduct towards the French capital.' In a similar vein, Field Marshal Blücher's timely appearance on the field of Waterloo three years later made Prussian motifs excessively popular with the middle classes.

Such overtly political symbolism was naturally accompanied by a widely expressed distaste for French fashions during the period 1793–1815. Yet,

Left: The Queen's Library at Frogmore, designed by Wyatt in 1803, as depicted in W. H. Pyne's Royal Residences *of 1819. Note the Regency carpet, the loose furniture covers, the muslin window-blind and the grained window joinery. None of the features shown here survive; accordingly, the room is being returned to its appearance of the early 1860s.*

Below: This interior from Lancaster House bears all the hallmarks of the latest and most expensive Regency fashions, with its rich red fabrics and sumptuous gilding. Lancaster House was extensively remodelled during the 1820s for the Duke of York – the brother of George IV and a widely-loathed reactionary whose dismal exploits during the French Wars were immortalized in the eponymous nursery rhyme. In fitting up the interiors the Duke almost matched the conspicuous extravagance of his brother at nearby Carlton House. Neither of these ostentatiously ambitious projects did much to endear the royal pair in the eyes of the general public.

given the reliance of designers such as Hope on contemporary French
Empire models, many followers of Regency fashion found themselves in an
embarrassing position. In 1805 the Regent himself told Lady Bessborough
that he was careful to avoid overt French elements at Brighton Pavilion,
'because at the time there was such a cry against French things, etc., that he
was afraid of his furniture being accused of Jacobinism'. Southey reflected the
general ambivalence towards France when he wrote of the English in 1807
that 'they hate the French and ape all their fashions . . . laugh at their
inventions and then adopt them'.

The conclusion of peace in 1815, however, brought French fashions
flooding back. In 1822 the *Repository* noted that 'The Taste for French
furniture is carried to such an extent, that most elegantly furnished mansions
. . . are fitted up in French style'. This enthusiasm became yet more fervent
following the fall of the restored Bourbon monarchy in 1830 and the
subsequent elevation of the liberal Anglophile Louis Philippe to the French
throne. At the same time Britain's increased prestige in Europe, epitomized
by the gains of the Treaty of Vienna and by the interventionist foreign policy
of Canning in the 1820s and Palmerston in the 1830s, helped foster a greater
confidence and pride in all things British.

Another fundamental characteristic of the Regency period which cannot
be ignored is the role of industrial development, and in particular the
mechanization of processes affecting interior design. The pace of
technological advance quickened rapidly after 1780. In 1785 steam was
harnessed to a cotton mill for the first time, and by 1788 there were forty
cotton mills in south Lancashire alone. By 1790 the cities of Liverpool, Hull,
Birmingham, Bristol, and London were all linked by canals, and in 1801
Richard Trevithick's steam carriage first appeared on the roads of Britain.
The effect of industrialization on traditional decorative and architectural
crafts was profound. At the beginning of the nineteenth century an observer
was writing that, 'It is impossible to contemplate the progress of
manufactures in Great Britain . . . without wonder and astonishment . . . The
improvement of the steam engines, but above all the facilities afforded to the
great branches of the woollen and cotton manufactories by ingenious
machinery, invigorated by capital skill, are beyond all calculation', particularly
as regards the 'silk, linen, hosiery, and various other branches' of the textile
trades. Housewives were now able to buy fabrics previously only affordable
by their betters; machine-printed textiles, advised Sheraton in 1794, could
now be 'adapted for the purpose of ornamenting panels and the walls of the
most elegant and noble houses' in every street. Rapid advances in dye
technology made the official ban on imported chintzes irrelevant.

Of course, technological progress was not limited to fabrics. Cylinder
presses replaced much of the hand-blocking of wallpapers; the appearance in
1839 of Harold Potter's power-driven rollers, able to print four colours and
to remove surplus ink, inaugurated the age of mass-produced wallpaper.
Similar innovations were introduced in almost every area of internal design:

Lucas Chance's plate glass of 1832 allowed window manufacturers more freedom to dispense with internal glazing bars; Samuel Bentham's woodworking machinery took much of the drudgery out of joinery mouldings; John Vickers' 'Britannia Metal' – an alloy of tin, copper, bismuth, and antimony – provided house owners with a cheap, malleable, and lustrous alternative to silver. The onset of war with France in 1793 provided a further boost to advances in the metalwork trades. Brass door furniture suddenly became widely available, while the forms of cast-iron door furniture grew more delicate and diverse. In 1805 Nash used cast-iron structural members, supplied by the Coalbrookdale Company, at the Attingham picture gallery; in 1816 J. C. Loudon invented the wrought-iron glazing bar; and in 1818 Nash was using a cage of iron ribs to form the basis for the onion domes of the Brighton Pavilion.

Brighton Pavilion at dusk.

Many innovations were designed expressly to make life more comfortable for the average householder. A good number helped to make houses warmer: Count Rumford's patent stove of 1796; steam heating, introduced by the Earl of Shelburne at Bowood during the 1790s and by Sir Walter Scott at Abbotsford in 1823; hot water piping, installed by the Duke of Wellington himself at Stratfield Saye in 1833. The Argand lamp helped illuminate the drawing room, while new gas lighting helped light the hallways – Lord Dundonald introduced it in his home in 1787 – and ultimately the streets – the first public gas lighting being installed in Pall Mall in 1807. Baths were a new fad, and by 1797 Joseph Bramah had sold 6,000 of his revolutionary ball-cock WC cisterns, patented in 1778. Nelson's house at Merton pointed the way forward in modern sanitation, with its astonishing disposition of one *en suite* bathroom attached to each of the five bedrooms. And house owners could now read about the newest technological advances: by 1800 there were 122 circulating libraries in London and 268 in the provinces, and over 250 periodicals to choose from.

Industrialization, and the growth of Britain's international role, also had the important effect of putting more money into the pockets of the middle classes. A Parliamentary report as early as 1806 noted that 'The rapid and prodigious increase of late years in the Manufactures and Commerce of this country is universally known, as well as the effects of that increase on our Revenue and National strength; and in considering the immediate causes of that Augmentation, it is principally ascribed to the general spirit of enterprise and industry.' As today, the principal reaction of the beneficiaries of this new prosperity was to transfer their wealth to bricks and mortar. The upper and middle classes of Regency Britain thus had a considerable amount of money to lavish on their homes. In the following chapters we shall see how they spent it.

AUGUSTUS AT ROME WAS FOR BUILDING RENOWNED AND OF MARBLE HE LEFT WHAT OF BRICK HE HAD FOUND. BUT IS NOT OUR NASH, TOO, A VERY GREAT MASTER? HE FINDS US ALL BRICK AND HE LEAVES US ALL PLASTER.

(ANON., 1826)

By 1800 the outward appearance and general internal disposition of the modest Regency house had become exceedingly familiar to most Britons – as well as to most Americans. Indeed, many of the basic building methods and practices used for the terrace housing of the later nineteenth century largely followed Late Georgian practice. The fact that the design of the terrace or of the unified street changed comparatively little throughout the Regency period was not wholly intentional: relatively few large-scale building projects were initiated during the era of the French Wars (1793–1815). However, the absence of any dramatic differences in style or approach was also due to the fact that builders and house owners alike found the typical Regency plan perfectly adequate, particularly at a time when the standards of craftsmanship and of industrial production had never been higher.

Urban housing during this period – and its rural counterpart, too – followed the same basic patterns as the houses of the previous sixty years, the principal difference in their façades being the type of facing materials employed. Late eighteenth-century innovations in room dispositions, such as the oval saloon or the circular hall, could rarely be accommodated within the cramped shells and meagre plots of most Regency homes. As John Summerson noted of the capital: 'Georgian London was a city made up almost entirely of . . . long narrow plots with their tall narrow houses and long narrow gardens or courts.' The result was, in Summerson's somewhat harsh and summary judgement, an 'inexpressible monotony' of housing developments. However, while much terrace housing of the period was not built to withstand great stresses or suffer copious alterations and depended considerably on interior partitions for structural integrity, architects and builders sought to combine the practical requirements of the typical, narrow

Exterior of Pitshanger Manor in west London, showing prolific use of yellow London stock bricks.

Nash's Regent Street, London, of 1818–20, seen in an engraving by T. H. Shepherd dated 1822, before its mutilation in the nineteenth and twentieth centuries.

Opposite: Tredegar Square, Bow, east London: a development of 1828 which ruined its ambitious builder, Daniel Austin. The yellow London stock bricks and the relieving arches around the windows are characteristic of the period. Originally, the ironwork would have been painted green or grey.

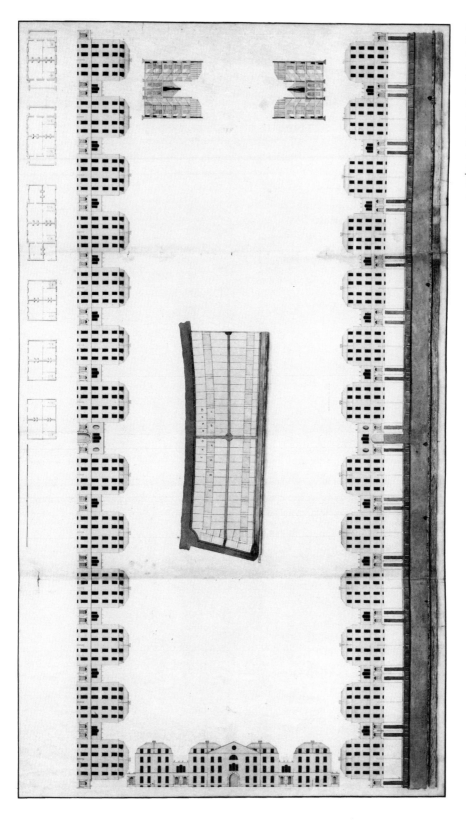

Michael Searles's unexecuted
design for 58 houses off Kent
Road in Southwark, south
London. The innovative format
of this projected development –
large semi-detached houses with
two-storey links – made for an
overall composition of far more
visual interest than the average
speculative terrace. Searles
adapted this idea for his
famous, executed scheme for the
Blackheath Paragon, begun in
1793.

George Cruikshank's view of Nash's dominance of the architectural world during the reign of George IV: Nash is impaled upon the spire of his own church of All Souls, Langham Place, London – part of his grand Regent's Park scheme.

Georgian house with the new air of informality and lightness wherever possible.

Passages between rooms were widened and walls less sharply defined. Double doors were by no means new; leaving them open for much of the day, however, was a daring innovation. In this way two rooms effectively became one – much in the manner of Soane's radical home in Lincoln's Inn Fields, where the ground-floor library was merged with the breakfast room, and the striking first-floor drawing room imperceptibly fused with the glazed street-front loggia. Humphry Repton strongly advocated the dismantling of small rooms and closets to create larger, more open spaces around which the furniture could now be moved freely. Large ground-floor sashes or French windows led directly to balconies, verandahs, or conservatories, providing a direct contact with nature and the outside world which would have been abhorrent to the earlier Georgians. As Repton noted in 1816:

whether the house be Grecian or gothic, large or small, it will require the same rooms for the present habits of life, viz. a dining-room and two others, one of which may be called a drawing-room, and the other a book-room, if small, or the library, if large: to these is sometimes added a breakfast room, but of late, especially since the central hall, or vestibule, has been in some degree given up, these rooms have been opened into each other, *en suite*, by large folding doors; the effect of this *enfilade*, or *visto*, through a modern house, is occasionally increased by a conservatory at one end, and repeated by a large mirror at the opposite end.

Of all the recent improvements to the small, modern house, Repton judged, 'none is more delightful than the connection of the living-rooms with a green-house or conservatory'. The opening of one room into another also afforded countless opportunites for misleading guests as to the true dimensions of modest interiors.

Outside, the principal elevations of the Regency terrace – or of the newly fashionable streets of grander, semi-detached homes – were still disposed according to the strict Palladian principles of proportion, first applied to British houses in the early eighteenth century. The austere Greek Neo-Classicism of Holland, Hope, and their followers made relatively little difference to the overall style of the run-of-the-mill Regency house, although isolated Greek motifs such as the acroterion – often reduced to simple plaster quarter-circle 'ears' adorning the doorcase or roof – or a Greek key pattern incised into the stucco did betray some superficial Neo-Classical influence. The principal developments in the façade – larger windows, simpler doorcases, stuccoed brickwork – were more often the result of technological advance or popular whim than derived from a sincere devotion to the forms of the antique world. Nash's and Cubitt's vast new estates of the 1820s were not so markedly different in their exteriors from their predecessors of the 1720s. Rectangular or perhaps round-headed sash windows dominated uniform, flat-roofed, and highly symmetrical terrace houses. To present an illusion of individual character and grandeur, the developer occasionally

Houses in Somerset Place, Bath, of 1790. The terrace here is faced in honey-coloured Bath stone, not in imitative stucco. Whenever the real thing was available, most architects forsook cheaper shams like painted stucco.

Opposite: Humphry Repton's before and after 'View from the fort, near Bristol' from his Observations . . . *of 1803, showing modern terraces integrated with the landscape.*

attached a redundant pediment, and perhaps a few pilasters, to the centrepiece of the composition; if the terrace was very pretentious or the developer simply wished to immortalize his own name, the title of the street or square would be proudly inserted into the middle of the pediment.

Of course, not every terrace was constructed to this straightforward pattern. Some of the more ambitious developments were envisaged not as straight streets but as crescents, a form popularized in the mid-eighteenth century by both John Wood the elder and the younger in Bath. Not that all Regency crescents are what they seem: Nash's famous Park Crescent in London, for example, was actually intended to be the southern half of a great circus, which was eventually extended northwards in the 1820s in more conventional fashion as Park Square. Nor was the Regency crescent necessarily a vast swathe of stucco. The impressive Pelham Crescent of 1824–8 in Hastings was of dour, grey, natural stone which blended well with the steep hillside into which it was so dramatically set. Even such a prominent landmark as fashionable Brighton's Royal Crescent of 1798–1807 was not faced with stucco but with the surprisingly humble, local medium of black mathematical tiles.

The Royal Crescent was of additional importance in representing, in Nairn and Pevsner's words, 'the earliest demonstration of a sympathy with the sea and beach'. In the popular new seaside towns builders and architects began to exploit the natural resources of sea, sand, air, and sunlight to the full, building three-sided squares and crescents open to the maritime breezes on their southern sides. A further variation was to experiment with the classic, flat Georgian façade. Houses in Brighton's Adelaide Square, for example, were given broad, elliptical bow fronts with which to catch the south-easterly sunlight. The fad for elliptical bays soon spread to the more modest streets which were multiplying along the seafront (humbler dwellings which, on account of their lower status, were invariably set at right-angles, not face-on, to the beach). If the builder could not afford to add rows of curved bays – or was not technically proficient enough – then a simple, three-sided projection would suffice.

The larger, detached homes of the period did, of course, allow for greater stylistic innovation. It was in these homes that the effects of the Greek, and later the Italianate, fashions were more keenly felt. Homes that were tailored more to individual clients than to a speculative template could naturally accommodate more exciting and daring structural features. Thus flatter 'Greek' arches became widespread, and more ingenious solutions were used internally to vault and light smaller spaces. Soane himself particularly favoured top-lit or domed vaults – and sometimes a combination of the two – and popularized the trend to flat, elliptical domes or arcades. The 'starfish' ceiling which Soane used to roof the breakfast room at his own home in London was an especially attractive and influential example of this solution.

The 1830s in particular witnessed a new exuberance in housing designed for the more prosperous middle classes. Gothic motifs appeared with

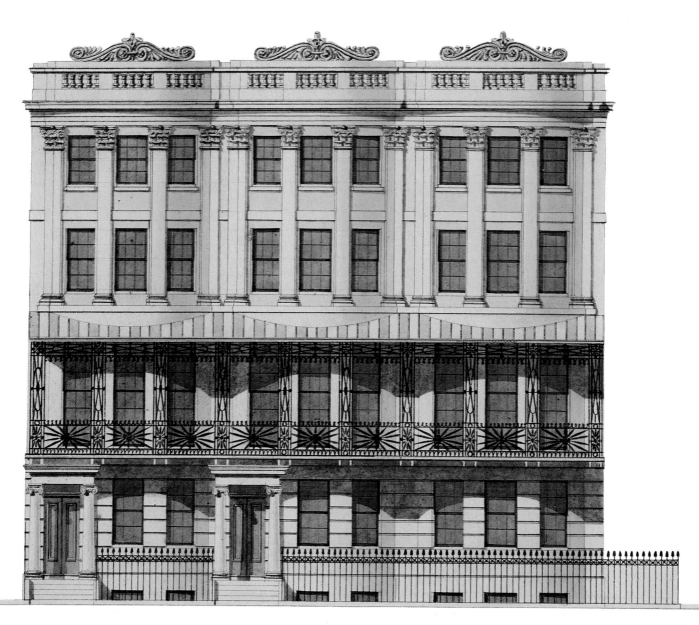

Brighton architect Charles Augustus Busby's design for a terrace in Brighton or Hove of the mid-1820s, possibly designed as part of his Brunswick Town development. Note the dark-painted window frames. Brunswick Town represents the climax of Busby's erratic career; always a difficult character, he fell out bitterly with his partner Amon Wilds in 1825, and though he continued to work in Brighton for the next nine years he saw countless key commissions in the town pass to his more politically amenable and temperamentally reliable rivals. Busby died almost penniless in 1834.

Opposite: Brunswick Square (top) and Regency Square (bottom) were both key elements in the new development of Brighton and its western neighbour, Hove, during the Regency period. The former was built by Busby and Wilds during the mid-1820s; the latter begun in 1818.

Neo-Classical caryatids adorn a building of the late 1830s in W. H. Knight's Montpellier Walk, at the heart of Regency Cheltenham. Not all the caryatids are of stone; some are painted terracotta.

Nash's Park Village West, London; completed after his death in 1835 by his adopted son and heir Sir James Pennethorne – whom, it was rumoured, may have been a bastard son of George IV. Note the widely projecting eaves of this Italianate tower-house – a fittingly modern and stylish home for the Regency nouveaux-riches.

increasing frequency after the craze for Gothic furniture took hold in the mid-1820s, though the Gothic style was still largely limited to pointed arches and windows inserted into what were still highly classical, regularly symmetrical frameworks, the academic fervour of the Victorian Gothicists being still some way off. For the more adventurous, pattern-books such as Loudon's impressively bulky *Encyclopaedia* of 1833 provided an immense array of inspirational plates of Gothic cottages, lodges, and interiors.

Yet it was the Italianate, 'Williamane' style which did most to liberate the wealthier middle-class house builders of the 1830s from the rigid precepts of Georgian housing. As Tim Mowl has pointed out, 'for just a few years, a light elegant Tuscan style . . . almost took over as the taste of the English suburbs'. Italianate, detached houses of this decade had a distinctly different profile from their Palladian or Neo-Classical forebears: Tuscan towers with heavy, deep cornices, closely-packed round-headed windows under the wide eaves, and most importantly, an asymmetric disposition, helped conjure a powerful and romantic silhouette for bankers' and merchants' villas in the most socially conservative of suburbs. This approach was first pioneered at Thomas Hope's own house at Deepdene in Surrey (1818–23) and rapidly caught on; by the late 1820s pattern-books were full of such towered designs, and by 1840 the new suburbs of Cheltenham, Bath, and Torquay were beginning to look distinctly Mediterranean. The powerful three-dimensionality of these compositions allowed for a far more imposing display of light and shadow than had been possible with the flat façades of the eighteenth century; these were romantic creations which quoted the poetic intensity of Shelley and Byron from the midst of planned suburban conventionality.

In the 1830s the architect Francis Goodwin noted that the new approach to suburban villa design 'tolerates many freedoms' and 'affects a certain unconstrained liveliness'. 'Tending towards the fanciful, if not the frivolous', he subsequently remarked, 'the style is far from being out of place where cheerfulness is the quality principally aimed at.' It is this 'cheerfulness' and romance which perhaps best characterizes the homes of the 1820s and 1830s; sadly, it is this aspect which is often forgotten when either house owners or even historians come to analyse the domestic architecture of this period.

Ostentatious, Byronic posturing was, of course, still only the prerogative of the wealthier sections of society. Only the simplest of Italianate motifs – projecting eaves, perhaps, or an elliptical arch or two – would find their way onto the façade of the average, speculatively built terrace. For this type of construction the governing principles were still cheapness and quickness. Whereas the threats of the Revolutionary and Napoleonic invasion fleets brought most large building projects to a halt in the early years of the century, by 1815 the pace of speculative building had comprehensively revived, and by 1820 vast areas of virgin land surrounding Britain's towns and cities were being sacrificed to the god of instant profit. Not all this development was in the guise of monotonous terrace, however. As fortunes

The astonishing Egyptian House in Penzance's Chapel Street, probably designed by John Foulston. Everything about this house is deliberately over the top: the huge overbearing cornice, the profuse octagonal glazing and the massive pillars all combine to assault the eye at once.

Ammonite capital of the mid-1820s in Montpellier Crescent, Brighton. The form of the capital was a pun on the name of the architect, Amon Wilds.

improved and pretensions increased, the better class of speculative housing was couched in the form of closely packed and identical, but nevertheless semi-detached, homes. As the social and financial aspiration of the development was raised, so were the gaps between the houses extended. The results were streets such as Michael Searles's Blackheath Paragon of *c*.1793: housing that, while effectively detached, still recalled the form of a terrace in its low, linking walls, its unfailing symmetry, and its repetitive uniformity.

This is not to say that all terrace housing was necessarily designed for leaseholders of lesser means. Nash's grand blocks bordering the Regent's Park were an avowed attempt to create an environment suitable for the *nouveaux riches*. As Nash himself stated: 'I have always been of the opinion that in forming the Regent's Park the buildings and even the Villas should be considered as Town residences not Country Houses. It is in the former character only we can expect the Houses will be occupied by the higher classes; to effect this the security of a contained and unbroken metropolis of Streets and Houses must be preserved.'

The basic structure of speculative terrace housing of the Regency period was strictly regulated by the provisions of the severe 1774 Building Act, a strict but effective piece of legislation which was often jokingly compared to the aptly named Coercive Acts of the same year, which did so much to provoke the American colonists. The aim of the act was both to raise building standards and to improve the levels of fireproofing – an understandable obsession which, over a hundred years after the Great Fire of London, was still remarkably strong. The act separated terrace housing into four categories or Rates, depending on the size and value of each house. A First Rate, for instance, was a house which possessed a rateable value of at least £850 a year and which amounted to over 900 square feet of floor space; at the other end of the scale, the Fourth Rater was valued at less than £150 p.a. and amounted only to 350 square feet. The act also laid down precise structural prerequisites for each Rate. No house was to feature any woodwork on the exterior save that necessary for the windows and doors; even then, window frames had to be largely recessed behind the masonry, and bow windows were barely allowed to project into the street.

Any examination of the Regency house must remain highly superficial if it ignores the basic materials used in constructing the architectural shell – a fundamental element so often dismissed purely as a clothes-horse for colours and textiles. The concept of 'Regency style' is not merely restricted to changes in fabrics and furniture; its evolution is evident in the use of even the most simple building materials.

Certainly the types of stone used for domestic masonry differed little from those employed during the preceding two centuries, being inevitably dependent on what was locally available. However, both technology and fashion did much to alter the colour and to some extent the function of brickwork during the period. Bricks were still made using the same basic elements, clay and sand. However, alongside the more primitive methods of

*Typical Regency brick forms
and patterns. Top row: reddish-
brown bricks laid in English
Garden Wall bond; yellow
London stocks (with later
inserts), in the far more
common Flemish bond
arrangement; cream-coloured
brickwork, designed to suggest
stone; second row: yellow
London stocks, plum-coloured
facing bricks and grey, vitrified
headers, all with contrasting
dressings in bright red brick;
third row: yellow mathematical
tiles; finely-made rubbed or
gauged red bricks, in straight
courses and made into a brick
arch, needing only the thinnest
of mortar joints; fourth row:
yellow and yellowish-grey
London stocks; bottom row:
rusticated stucco, applied to hide
the cheap brickwork behind;
tuck pointing; and black, salt-
glazed mathematical tiles.*

Cruikshank's cartoon 'Bricks and mortar going out of London' aptly sums up the pace of urban development in Regency England.

Various types of rustication suitable for stone or stucco walls, as recommended by J. C. Loudon in his magisterial Encyclopaedia of Cottage, Farm and Villa Architecture of 1833. These range from straightforward incised jointing to 'surfaces punctured in imitation of rude rock'.

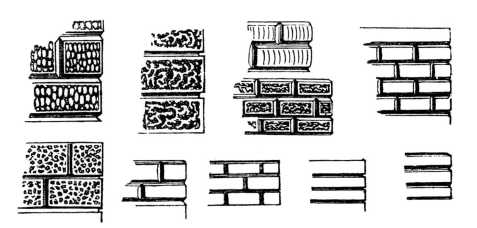

firing bricks – clamps with fire-holes or scotch kilns (effectively clamps with permanent brick walls) – now appeared more sophisticated kilns, fired not with the traditional combustive materials – wood, charcoal, bracken or heather – but with the fuel of the industrial revolution, coal. At the same time paler brick colours became highly fashionable. These shades were designed to recall stone rather than the humble Early Georgian red brick, which was more often relegated to brick arches or dressings. Henry Holland popularized the use of cream-coloured 'Suffolk whites' in the 1770s, using white bricks, and not stone or even stucco, for the grand front façade of Brooks's Club in London's fashionable St James's.

As London expanded again after 1810, so brickfields sprang up all over the capital and the south-east. The local clays in these areas often produced a characteristically yellow or yellow-grey brick known as a 'London stock'. The term 'stock' was actually quite meaningless: the 'stock board' was originally the base on which wholly hand-made bricks were moulded; a 'stock brick', however, had by 1780 come to mean any brick of average shape and strength – also collectively known as 'commons' – which could be used not for fine, precise work or for exposed parapets or walls but for terrace façades and other relatively undemanding tasks. The coal-firing of kilns now produced a greater range of brick colours, the greater heat obtained in the hottest parts of the kiln burning the raw bricks far more effectively than before.

Outside London many brickworks found they could get a much wider range of colours from their local clays – the chemical composition of the clay was now vital in determining how broad a colour range could be obtained – and discovered that they no longer had to rely solely on the traditional red varieties which had been their mainstay in previous years. Greater heat efficiency in the kiln also allowed for the easier production of blue-grey, 'vitrified' bricks. These were placed adjacent to the fire-holes in the clamp so that the intense heat, reacting with the lime in the clay, produced a glazed effect on the brick's surface. They could now be used not only to form the traditional 'chessboard' walls – where vitrified headers alternated with red stretchers – but, owing to their increased availability and lower price, to form whole façades on their own. If the brick was still not deemed pale enough after firing, then a more accurate 'stone colour' could be obtained by limewashing the brick to give it a whiter sheen. In 1803 Humphry Repton explicitly recommended a stone-coloured wash for brickwork in order to disguise the 'meanness' of red bricks.

In September 1784, to help pay for the recent, ruinous American War, a brick tax of 2s. 6d. per thousand was imposed on all bricks. Despite much popular mythology, this failed to have a drastic effect on brick prices; nevertheless, subsequent tax increases in 1794 and 1803 – again to pay for a war, this time against the French – did not do much to aid a brick trade already affected by the slump in speculative building projects. The revival in residential building was swift, however, and – in spite of the continuation of the tax, only finally repealed in 1850 – the fortunes of the brickmakers

Brighton's Royal Crescent of 1798–1807. Built on the seafront, the houses are faced not, as it first appears, with bricks, but with glazed black mathematical tiles – a traditional local material.

*Loudon's diagrams illustrate
how 'the Walls of Cottages may
be protected by Mathematical
Tiling'. He shows different
lengths of tile, and how the tiles
appear – in section and in
elevation – when laid. Below is
a row of ornamental weather
tiles, from the same source.*

soared. By the 1830s brickmaking machines were in widespread use, producing bricks faster and cheaper to cope with the new demand for homes; these shaped the bricks mechanically, using either a simple press for individual bricks or an extrusion process in which a continuous brick shape was forced out of the end of the machine, rather like toothpaste being squeezed from a tube.

Another myth connected with the brick tax was that in 1784 an overnight demand was created for mathematical tiles, tiles with large pegs at the rear which, when nailed onto wooden laths in overlapping layers, resembled brick courses. Mathematical tiles had actually been in use since the seventeenth century, most notably in Kent and Sussex, and indeed were also subject to a levy (of 3s. per thousand) by the Act of 1784. And as the colours of bricks changed during the period, so did those of their imitators. Grey, white, and yellow tiles were widely used in the fashionable Sussex towns of Brighton and Lewes; black, glazed mathematical tiles, designed to mimic the salt-glazed brickwork of the area, were applied to the front elevations of Brighton's Royal Crescent. Such mimicry, though, can rarely pass wholly undetected: the surface of the completed tiling was never as uniformly flat as that of a brick wall, although the resultant effects of reflected light are possibly even more attractive; additionally, the tiles were unable to encompass right angles, and thus the corner of a mathematically tiled house was generally fitted with a painted board (sometimes metamorphosed into a fully fledged pilaster) to terminate the tile courses neatly.

The Regency brick trade was kept remarkably healthy not only by the

Sir John Soane's small but perfectly formed Dulwich Picture Gallery of 1811–14 included the very latest Regency building fashions: bright yellow stock brickwork, incised render, and Greek motifs used both inside and out.

new demand for light-coloured common or specialist products, but also by the speculative builders' need for large quantities of inferior brickwork – not for the façades, but to act as the basic wall structure, as well as a plaster key, for the stuccoed terraces which were so prevalent by the end of the period. The whole family of external renders – stuccoes, mastics, Roman cements, 'Portland' cements – developed considerably during the Regency. Stucco is essentially a thin render, a mixture based principally on lime and sand, which was commonly applied to a wall in three coats in an attempt to disguise inferior masonry as finely dressed blocks of ashlar. It became the hallmark of the Regency terrace and was in essence simply an imitative material – like graining or marbling, those other popular illusory devices beloved of Regency designers. The Italians had devised the term 'stucco' to denote a mix of powdered marble and lime; in eighteenth-century Britain, however, the term was being used for any type of internal or external plasterwork, and it was only in the early nineteenth century that it came specifically to signify *exterior* rendering of the type designed to suggest fine stonework. It was never, however, intended to serve as anything other than a cheap sham. Nash always conceived his streetscapes in terms of genuine Bath stone – stucco was simply far cheaper – and when he was able to use the real thing (at Buckingham Palace, for example), he did.

Not all stuccoes were of admirable quality or composition. In 1797 William Marshall's *Rural Economy of Gloucestershire* observed that: 'The scrapings of the public roads; namely, levigated limestone, impregnated more or less with the dung and urine of the animals travelling upon them, are found to be an excellent basis for cement.' Yet during the 1770s the Adam brothers had done much to promote stucco by utilizing James Liardet's oil-based stucco or mastic for their Adelphi scheme and for Kenwood House. The ensuing enthusiasm for Liardet's product was quickly dissipated, however, by the surprising discovery that Britain's climate was somewhat less clement than that of Italy, whence stucco had originated, and the subsequent realization that oil-based stuccoes were highly unreliable and prone to failure. The result was that by 1780 Liardet's stucco was falling off houses all over London.

Yet the failure of Liardet's recipe did not deter the greatest practitioner of the stuccoed terrace, John Nash. In 1796 the Reverend James Parker temporarily abandoned his clerical duties to patent 'Parker's Roman Cement'. So-called 'Roman Cements' bear little relation to modern cements but were, in fact, quick-setting renders based on hydraulic lime, made from limestone containing a good proportion of clay. This, when combined with water or reactive materials such as pulverized fuel ash, produced a quick-setting and cheap stucco. In 1812 Nash was specifying Parker's Roman Cement at his ambitious Park Crescent development and proceeded to plaster it over many of his Regent's Park terraces.

By 1830 examples of stucco could be seen on most of the fashionable terraces of Regency Britain. Even the Regent's Brighton Pavilion could boast the prominent use of the material –in this case 'Dehl's Mastic', patented in 1815 and used to cover the massive onion domes. As at many other sites, however, this stucco proved excessively troublesome, the turpentine and linseed oil base tending to crack when dry. Answering the charge that 'It has been represented to His Majesty that the Dehl Mastic employed on the roofs, has *completely failed*', in 1822 Nash bravely alleged 'that *I know* the Mastic in a *perfect state* to be *impervious to wet*'. Yet the domes continued to crack and crumble. Partly to excuse both Nash and Dehl, though, it is worth adding that the replacement of the mastic domes with fibreglass replicas in the 1960s proved considerably more disastrous, since the new domes failed dramatically after a bare fifteen years.

Technology, however, soon made all these simple stuccoes obsolete. The manufacture of a harder render, now known as 'artificial cement', was first successfully attempted in Britain in 1811. Thirteen years later the Leeds bricklayer Joseph Aspdin patented his 'Portland Cement' – so called because of the alleged similarity of the finished product to Portland stone. While this is not very similar to modern Portland cement, and although the reliability of Aspdin's own product was actually rather poor, subsequent improvements had made artificial cements extremely popular by the 1850s. But the death-knell for stucco had not been sounded by industrial progress alone. By 1840 the whole fashion for stucco was waning, its demise hastened not only by the material's proven unreliability but also by the inimical attitude of the new generation of Gothic Revival architects such as A. W. N. Pugin, who violently denounced stucco as a sham product of the debased Classical age.

Most stucco was intended to be painted. Yet the light cream tones we inevitably associate with stucco terraces today are actually a mid-nineteenth-century innovation. Regency stucco was often coloured far darker than it is now, designed as it was to reflect the hues of the local stone. In 1833 J. C. Loudon's *Encyclopaedia* recommended that: 'The kinds of colours suitable for exterior walls should generally be such as belong to the stones or bricks of the country. These are chiefly whites, browns, yellows and reds.' More importantly, stuccoed terraces were always conceived as unified compositions both in terms of style and colour. As Nash stated: 'If a unity in the character of the houses can be preserved so as to exhibit the entirety of a single building, its commanding situation will produce an effect of grandeur in the greatest degree striking.' Thus, even if today the colour of the stucco no longer resembles that of the original façade, the same colour should always be adopted for the whole of the terrace or block. These days responsible local authorities such as Hove and Westminster Councils actually stipulate the precise paint to be used on stuccoed surfaces; this helps to avoid unsympathetic, 'individual' interpretations of adjoining houses. Originally, too, the incised lines suggesting stone joints were often enhanced by painted grey 'shadows'. Loudon suggested using the technique of paint 'splashing': 'either to imitate the lichens and weather stains of an old wall, or some particular kind of stone'. Such meticulous *trompe-l'œil* detail has, alas, often

The iron-framed, mastic-covered domes of Nash's remodelling of Brighton Pavilion.

Opposite, top: Charles Tomkins's view of 1798 of Eleanor Coade's 'Coade Stone' factory in Pedlar's Acre, Lambeth.

Opposite, below: A Coade Stone urn in the Great Hall at Temple Newsam near Leeds. The house was redecorated in the late 1820s by George IV's discarded mistress, Lady Hertford.

disappeared without trace beneath layers of crude modern paint.

Stucco's poor record of durability in tougher climes made it a bad material with which to execute precise detailing. During the Regency period, however, external detailing of an astonishing strength was achieved through the use of the new invention Coade Stone, which, despite its title, was actually a hard-wearing ceramic. The impressive businesswoman Eleanor Coade managed her Lambeth manufactory so successfully in the years following its foundation in 1769 that by 1800 there was a permanent exhibition of Coade works established on Westminster Bridge. Mrs Coade underlined the quality of her products by engaging the celebrated sculptor John Bacon to design some of the more ambitious Coade pieces. Unfortunately, though, the factory barely survived the death of her daughter in 1821, and Coade Stone remains a phenomenon almost entirely restricted to the Regency period. Today the detail of most Coade pieces is still as crisp as when they were made. Unsurprisingly, it was a material quickly seized upon by more far-sighted designers such as John Soane. Soane's bronzed Coade figures in the parlour at Pitshanger Manor – the Ealing house he built for his sons – not only represent the epitome of Regency 'sham' decoration but also display the remarkable longevity of Mrs Coade's ceramic. It is always worth checking whether a Regency plaque, statue, or tablet, apparently of

stone or plaster, is actually a Coade piece; the luckier detectives will find
a Coade inscription on the base which should give the game away.

Perhaps the most fundamental effect of Britain's gallop towards
industrialization on domestic building projects was the introduction of
structural ironwork. In 1802 the French architect Bélanger noted that the
British 'have been the first to substitute cast iron in order to supplement
stone and carpentry', while in 1818 the architect J. B. Papworth noted that
'The manufacture of iron has been greatly benefitted by improvements in the
art of casting it' and that 'iron itself is now at a very reduced price'. Much of
the grace, lightness, charm, and virtuosity of the Regency house derives not
through decoration alone but is a direct result of the vastly increased
possibilities that the use of iron encouraged. Load-bearing timbers began to
be replaced by cast-iron beams in the 1790s, and by 1820 houses of all types
had their floors and ceilings supported by iron girders which, being stronger
as well as less prone to decay than timber, freed more space for less purely
functional ends. Designers were also quick to appreciate the fire-resistant
qualities of iron. In 1792 a committee of distinguished architects – including
Holland, Revett, Chambers, Soane, and Wyatt – specially constructed two
houses in order to test rival theories of fire prevention. The following year
they recommended the provision of metal plates and beams in all floors and
ceilings.

While timber was by no means banished from the home, the new-found
strength of the iron-framed house allowed for more daring internal and
external planning. Balconies could be extended out on the garden front: wide
and spacious, this newly fashionable first-floor feature was supported not
simply on the brackets visible on the underside but, in fact, by iron girders
which extended far into the house. Staircases could now be cantilevered out –
apparently unsupported – from load-bearing walls, over ground-floor spaces
now freed for alternative uses. In 1815 Nash installed the celebrated 'bamboo
staircase' at Brighton Pavilion. This structure was wholly of cast iron: not
only the balusters (cast and painted to imitate real bamboo) but also the
treads, stringers, risers, and handrails. Iron framing was subsequently used by
Nash for the first-floor rooms leading off this stair; thus, whatever the
fragility of Nash's decorative domes, the Pavilion's basic structure has proved
strong and secure enough to withstand whatever the twentieth century has
thrown at it – whether bombs, hurricanes, or Molotov cocktails.

The manufacture of cast iron received its biggest boost in 1794, the year
Wilkinson's 'cupola' was invented. This was essentially a small blast furnace
for remelting pig iron, and it was able to produce cast iron quickly and
cheaply. (The production of steel, however – an attempt to re-create wrought
iron in a similarly commercially efficient manner – was not successfully
achieved until the 1850s.) Cast iron allowed for greater repetition at a low
price; improved casting techniques also allowed for more precision and
definition. Equally importantly, iron's inherent strength allowed architects to
design in a lighter vein, a development which in turn helped foster the

General view and detail, left, of curved iron glazing bars from the Picture Gallery at Attingham, Shropshire, built by Nash in 1807. The introduction of the curved iron glazing bar revolutionized Regency roof and conservatory design, allowing for far more graceful and ambitious glass structures.

*T. H. Shepherd's view of villas
in Nash's Park Village East,
London, of 1824–8. Note the
pronounced eaves and other
Italianate references.*

increasing informality of the Regency house. No longer did domestic function and family leisure have to be sacrificed to the overriding goal of structural stability. Humphry Repton advocated the use of iron not just to mimic more traditional materials and dispositions but to create 'many beautiful effects of lightness' while a sales catalogue of 1793 confidently declared that: 'The change now taking place in the materials for sashes, skylights, fan-lights, staircases &c. &c. from Wood to Metal has, besides the elegance of appearance, the advantages of strength and extensive durability.'

From the 1780s windows were constructed that were no longer made of softwood but of iron, with internal glazing bars of cast iron, brass, copper, or even bronze. (The effect of this on the size and configuration of the Regency window is analysed in the chapter below.) External railings could now be lighter in weight, allowing for greater patterning and elaboration. Traditional spear- or javelin-headed railings were supplemented by elaborate friezes and vertical panels featuring typical Greek ornament, by delicate scrolling that recalled the great, fabulously expensive works of the late seventeenth century, and by expertly cast urn finials with characteristic, finely detailed acorn tops.

In some houses cast iron also began to replace leadwork for downpipes, gutters, and hoppers. While iron gutters have proved reliable, however, iron for lead hoppers has often been an unfortunate substitution, which has resulted in rusting and eventual failure. Lead was still the preferred material for such services and, given its malleability, one that was easily adaptable to changes in fashion and technology.

By the 1830s the pace of technological change was even affecting the roof of the house. Lead had traditionally been used for the unseen, low-pitched or valley-gutter roofs which inevitably surmounted the typical Regency terrace or parapeted villa. However, light and durable zinc roofing sheets, first commercially produced in Belgium in 1811, began to appear on British roofs during the 1830s, either in tile or sheet form. At the same time light copper sheeting began to be used for roofing and cladding. Such metals, however, never widely displaced the well-established roofing materials. Even the more radically planned Gothic cottages of the 1820s and 1830s, with their traditional pitched roofs, did not abandon traditional slate, stone, or clay roofing tiles. It was only at the end of the nineteenth century that cement technology had progressed sufficiently far to enable a concrete tile – of the type now disfiguring so many of Britain's period homes – to be successfully manufactured.

THE WINDOWS, TO WHICH SHE LOOKED WITH PECULIAR DEPENDENCE, FROM HAVING HEARD THE GENERAL TALK OF HIS PRESERVING THEM IN THEIR GOTHIC FORM WITH REVERENTIAL CARE, WERE YET LESS WHAT HER FANCY HAD PORTRAYED. TO BE SURE, THE POINTED ARCH WAS PRESERVED ... BUT EVERY PANE WAS SO LARGE, SO CLEAR, SO LIGHT!

(JANE AUSTEN,
Northanger Abbey, 1817)

St Andrew's Place, London, built in the mid-1820s as part of Nash's scheme for the east side of the new Regent's Park. The original colour of the painted stucco would have been considerably darker, the window frames would have been painted brown or grained, and the ironwork would most probably have been painted green.

Windows are invariably the aspect of the house's exterior that is noticed first. They are effectively the eyes of a building, and any major alteration in their form or colour significantly alters the disposition of the façade. By the Regency period their role had become doubly important since, in response to advances in glass technology, windows were occupying more and more of the wall space. Of course, as well as constituting the most visually immediate part of the house, they also remained, in an age of endemic violence, its Achilles' heel. During the rioting over Parliamentary reform in 1831, for example, the diarist and inveterate gossip Princess Lieven laconically noted that 'The [anti-Reform] Tories refused to illuminate – so all the windows of their houses were broken by the mob, and they were forced to sleep in fresh air.'

Developments in glass technology inevitably did most to alter the form of the window after 1790. During the eighteenth century glass was generally made in one of two ways. 'Crown glass', the best quality product, was made by spinning out a blown globe of molten glass – making, in the words of one contemporary observer, 'a loud ruffling noise, like the rapid unfurling of a flag in a strong wind' – to form a disc not exceeding five or possibly six feet in diameter. This was then rested on a bed of sand, disengaged from the rod (or 'pontil'), and after cooling was cut into panes, the size of which could economically be no more than 10″ by 15″. 'Cylinder', 'broad', or 'muff' glass was made by swinging the molten glass over a pit to lengthen it; the resulting

An illustration from Diderot's Encyclopédie *of crown-glass manufacturing in the late eighteenth century.*

Opposite: How not to paint a stuccoed terrace: Neapolitan ice-cream effects applied to Nash's Park Square West, London, of 1823–6. Stuccoed terraces such as this one were always conceived by their designers as single, unified entities, not as a succession of jarringly individual dwellings.

cylinder was then opened out – being reheated over a metal plate covered in sand – and cut up into panes of rather more indifferent quality than was achieved by the crown method.

Old glass, particularly crown glass, is irreplaceable, especially since no British firm now produces it – although some do manufacture tolerable substitutes. Every effort should be made to retain it where it exists: its faint greenish colour, its bell-like sound, and above all its marvellous oscillations and regular imperfections, which catch the light so beautifully, contrast dramatically with the dull, characterless uniformity of modern glass. If you are restoring old windows, make sure, then, that the glass is not unnecessarily replaced; so much crown or cylinder glass, despite initial assurances to the contrary from the builder, ends up simply being thrown away.

By 1830 traditional glass-making methods had been refined so as to allow for larger panes to be cut from the discs or cylinders. In 1832, however, the industry was irreversibly transformed: Lucas Chance began to produce a markedly improved form of cylinder glass at his factory in Stourbridge, using new continental techniques to produce the first 'plate' glass. This new, more standardized product revolutionized the industry and enabled the production of far larger and more uniform panes. Significantly, it was Chance Brothers who, nineteen years later, were to be contracted to supply the glass for the Crystal Palace.

Innovations in glass-making had immediate repercussions for the window-making trades, since windows could now be constructed which needed far fewer glazing bars to support the vulnerable glass. Thick and heavy glazing bars were very much a thing of the past, as glazing bar profiles became more slender and graceful – often carved in the ever-popular 'lamb's tongue' or 'gothic' configurations. The introduction of stronger, metal glazing bars in the 1820s allowed for even fewer internal window supports. The result was that the characteristic mid-Georgian sash window, usually of six-over-six or eight-over-eight panes, was gradually replaced by windows, larger in size, comprising four-over-four or even two-over-two panes. The introduction of plate glass meant that by 1840 sash windows were being made which needed no internal glazing at all. As a structural precaution, though, 'horns' were introduced at the corners of the meeting rails. Extensions of the stiles (the principal side members), they were designed specifically to strengthen the frames; they do not – as is often the practice with reproduction windows today – need to be added to Georgian windows, which have sufficient internal glazing bars to support the glass.

In houses already built, as well as in new homes, window sills were often lowered and new windows installed which extended right down to the skirting or even the ground. These not only let in more light; in keeping with the new air of informality which so characterized the Regency house, floor-length windows were used to diminish the sense of division between the inside of the home and the outside and to encourage the occupants and their guests to wander freely in and out, without the necessity of using the door.

A round-headed window with thin, delicate glazing bars from Thomas Jefferson's Monticello, Virginia. Jefferson designed this house for himself; building work began in 1770 but the house was totally reconstructed, to its present form, between 1796 and 1808. In plan Monticello is remarkably similar to the villas of Robert Taylor.

Typical windows of the early nineteenth century. Top row: round-headed sash with large panes; window with margin lights; second row: two eight-over-eight sashes with stuccoed surrounds of the mid-1830s; bottom row: early iron window, the lower sash frame of which can be propped open to allow access to the garden; large-paned sash with fine iron window-guard. Opposite; top row: sashes set into stuccoed terraces of the 1820s; second row: window from Monticello, with its original crown glass; crown glass visible in a window at Ephrata Cloister, Pennsylvania; bottom row: margin lights in a fine window of the 1830s – behind which the shutters have, sadly, been stripped; a bay of c.1820 in Ambrose Place, Worthing, Sussex.

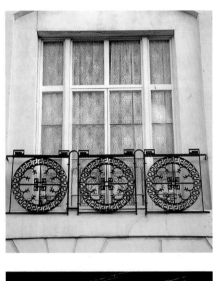

Nature hides the architectural form: clematis trailed over a Hampstead villa of 1807. The windows are very much of the period: long and tall, with narrow margin lights.

Gothic glazing in Ely, Cambridgeshire.

To this end the bottom sashes of floor-length windows were often able to be propped open permanently (safely, so as to avoid the ghastly fate of Sterne's Tristram Shandy a half-century before: 'Susannah did not consider that nothing was well-hung in our family – so slap came the sash down like lightning upon us.'); they could be either securely fastened when pulled up or dropped into a specially constructed hole below the ground. In 1807 Robert Southey's fictional Spanish commentator Don Manuel Espriella, of his *Letters from England*, declared that: 'Nothing surprised me more at first, than the excellent workmanship of the doors and windows; no jarring with the wind, no currents of air, and the windows, which are all suspended by pulleys, rise with a touch.' The natural progression from the extension of the window area was to convert the floor-length window into a glazed door – hence the 'French window', an innovation which, despite its name, was not especially French at all. Floor-length windows or glazed doors were particularly used to give access into the garden at the rear of the house, or onto newly fashionable features such as the ground-floor conservatory or first-floor verandah. Jane Austen's *Persuasion* (published in 1818, but written two or three years before) testifies to the popularity of this arrangement, eulogizing 'Uppercross Cottage, with its Viranda, French windows, and other prettiness'.

Whereas the panes of Regency windows were larger than before, visual interest was frequently retained by the device of inserting margin lights, narrow panes placed at the borders of the glazing. These were often of coloured glass – pink, lilac, blue, or amber. Indeed, coloured glass became a feature of many Regency homes; Sir John Soane in particular delighted in using amber glass throughout the windows of his house in London, thereby flooding the interior with glowing, radiant yellow light.

Another fancy, especially during the 1820s and 1830s, was the use of octagonal or, more commonly, Gothic glazing. 'Gothic' windows – which were not (unlike later in the century) designed to be exact facsimiles of medieval examples and were, in fact, inserted into highly Classical contexts – were quite the height of fashion by 1830. They reflected the new sense of aesthetic freedom, as house owners sought to escape from the rigid strait-jackets of Palladian or Neo-Classical taste which had been so rigorously imposed during the preceding century. The passion for Gothic gradually filtered down not only from the prosaic plates of Ackermann and other contemporary pattern-books but also from romantic extravagances such as Wyatt's notorious Fonthill Abbey: built for the fabulously wealthy homosexual recluse William Beckford between 1796 and 1812, Fonthill's fantastic central tower, 276 feet high, collapsed spectacularly a bare thirteen years after the house's completion – taking most of the rest of the Abbey with it.

One myth about Regency fenestration, however, definitely needs exploding. The bow window was certainly much used throughout this period, particularly in seaside towns such as Brighton, where it was used to catch the

Far left: 'Protected fixed canopies . . . for giving consequence to windows' from Loudon's Encyclopaedia *of 1833. Left: window dressings from the same publication – 'fine sources of character for windows and doors' which, 'when properly and not too profusely introduced in an elevation', gave an 'excellent' effect.*

*Blind boxes and balconies of the
mid-1820s in Hove's
impressively stuccoed Brunswick
Square, a square dominated by
the large full-height bays.*

sunlight radiating from the sea. Inland, though, it was more often used as a device to front ground-floor shops than to display the wares of non-commercial householders. Even then, the 1774 Building Act stipulated that bay windows should project no further into the street than ten inches – less in narrower lanes. Most importantly, the 'bottle-glass bow' window, a feature so beloved of the purveyors of modern mock-Georgian and so frequently associated with the Regency, never truly existed. 'Bottle glass' or, more properly, 'bullion' panes were actually inferior by-products of the manufacture of crown glass, cut from the point of the spun circle where the glassblower's pontil had been affixed and later removed. Since glass remained an expensive commodity, even the centre of the crown circle was used; but most often the resulting pane was confined to windows which would never be glimpsed by passers-by: rear or kitchen windows, or perhaps modest internal doors leading into the kitchen. 'Bottle-glass' was never used on front elevations. There is evidence, too, that these panes can represent serious fire hazards: the 'bottle-glass' indentation can concentrate the sun's rays in the manner of a magnifying glass and can actually set alight the curtains behind the window.

Some bay windows were, of course, simple casements. The sash window, however, remained the quintessential form for the English window throughout the Regency; aside from their frequent use in America, and occasional use in Holland, sashes remained peculiar to Britain. As during the eighteenth century, Regency sashes were invariably fitted with interior shutters; indeed, they were now of even more importance in retaining heat and light, since many of the curtains of the time were fixed drapery displays, never intended to be operated. (Many house owners are unaware that they still possess workable shutters inside their shutter boxes. It is always worth checking this before you embark on complicated draught-proofing or secondary glazing.) Exterior shutters were also to be found; most, though, have now been dismantled, and only their fixtures survive as a record. External roller blinds, too, were decidedly popular during the Regency period. These were drawn up into painted wooden blind boxes, but while the boxes often survive – used as shades for the sun – it is extremely rare to find an extant exterior blind. From the evidence we do have, it seems that they were made of very heavy-duty canvas and were often decorated in gaily-coloured stripes.

Technological advances even affected the mechanisms within the sash boxes. In sophisticated houses rope sash cords were, from the 1820s onwards, replaced with tougher metal chains. More commonly, wooden sash pulleys – the rule for windows until the 1760s – were discarded in favour of longer-lasting examples made of brass or cast iron. Window furniture became more profuse and more elaborate as brass and other alloys became cheaper and more widely available, and the fitting of devices such as sash fasteners became the rule rather than the exception.

Window colours – always a topical subject with keen decorators – varied

Above: Hartland's marvellous, if a little impractical, 'Device for moving houses' ('As adopted in the United States by Letters Patent') of 1833. The green-painted shutters and the general window treatments are particularly interesting. Unfortunately, external shutters such as these rarely survive today.

Right: A view of the Little Theatre, Haymarket, London, of c.1800, showing grey-painted window joinery and green-painted front doors.

far more than is often believed. For much of the eighteenth century, window joinery had been painted white or another light colour. (Georgian 'white', of course, was never akin to the bright, bleached whites so amenable to modern tastes; these stark whites remain very much a product of the twentieth century, being far too strident and dominating to be used on historical façades. Georgian whites were nearly always 'broken' – mixed with a tiny proportion of darker paint to give a richer effect; the result was often called not simply 'white' but 'stone colour'.) By the 1780s, however, some windows, particularly when in the context of painted stucco, were painted in darker hues. The architect John Yenn employed dark-grey painted windows in a villa design of 1769, while William Chambers used grey windows at Somerset House in London a few years later. By 1800 darker greys and browns were surprisingly popular for fashionable homes. Soane frequently used dark painted sashes, while the leases of Nash's Regent's Park development specifically called for the repainting of the windows in a brown, imitation oak graining every four years. Green, too, was used for Regency window joinery, particularly in rural 'cottages ornés' and other products of the taste for the Picturesque. Jane Austen's *Sense and Sensibility* of 1811 condemned Barton Cottage for the fact that 'the window shutters were not painted green'. Twenty-five years later Dickens in *Pickwick Papers* was observing that: 'the chief features in the still life of the street are green shutters, lodging-bills, brass door-plates, and bell handles'. Many of these darker colours were overpainted with cream as a result of the late nineteenth-century fashion for the chaste 'Queen Anne' style, and very few have survived the twentieth century's rather disturbing passion to have everything whiter than white. Where there is no evidence for a darker colour, however, it is perhaps better to play safe and use a broken white for window joinery.

Opposite: A federal door in Chestnut Street, Salem, Massachusetts, of the 1790s. The six vertically-arranged panels are particularly interesting; the low, Adam-style fanlight harks back to the fashions of twenty years before.

Typical doors of the 1820s and 30s from Essex Road and Tredegar Square, London. Note the fanlights – variants on the typically Regency 'teardrop' or 'batswing' patterns. Reeded jambs and low fanlights are redolent of this period, as is dark paintwork. By 1830 door numbers would have been commonly found in the larger cities.

Old front doors have, in recent years, been much abused, yet they are of fundamental importance as the focus of any domestic façade. Door patterns of the period varied enormously, but the most characteristic Regency front door was not of the six-panelled arrangement so common in the eighteenth century but of two or three panels, disposed either horizontally or vertically. The mouldings on the exterior of the front door were simpler than before, but more profuse. Often, multiple bead mouldings – 'reeded surrounds', a motif highly typical of the Regency period – were used to define the edges of the panels, with paterae (each inset with a circular panel or similar motif) emphasizing the corners. On occasion the panels were enriched with inset or raised circles or diamonds – all, again, strongly defined by their reeded surrounds – or were, in the case of doors with two vertical panels, given rounded heads. Soane liked to emphasize front-door panels by placing raised studs around their edges, an innovation which found favour among some of his contemporaries, too. The traditional six-panelled door, however, was not wholly ignored. This form, with the small rectangular panels positioned either at the top or in the middle of the front door, continued to be used throughout the nineteenth century. The two bottom panels of these multi-panelled doors were frequently fused together and raised flush with the surrounding members, so as to provide a thicker surface more resilient to impatient feet. In contrast with the other panels, this flush area was connected to the adjacent stiles and rails by a simple, single bead moulding.

Whereas the door itself was growing more elaborate, however, the Regency doorcase was becoming increasingly less pretentious than its Georgian forebears. Gone were the elaborate pedimented or hooded porches which projected so dramatically into the street or drive; gone were the imposing sets of flanking columns and pilasters; gone were the vast Adam fanlights, filled with delicate, spidery tracery, which spanned the entire width of the doorcase and adjacent windows. In contrast, the typical Regency doorcase was flat, compact, and restrained. Instead of boldly projecting columns, reeded architraves – resembling engaged columns which exhibited only a quarter of their surface to the air – shouldered the door. Even when these architraves metamorphosed back into true columns or pilasters, with identifiable capitals, they were still deliberately left understated. And, whether an architrave or columns, the surround generally tended to support only a reeded lintel or simple fanlight.

Fanlights, too, were far less elaborate than in Adam's day. The complex and delicate tracery arrangements of the 1770s had by 1800 largely been replaced with more prosaic designs, based on simple geometric shapes, or a form particularly characteristic of the early nineteenth-century doorcase – serpentine curves. The size of the fanlight had been reduced, back to the width of the door alone, and by the 1820s flat arches in the Greek manner were more common above the doorway than grand semicircular spans. By 1840 the fanlight had become quite unfashionable; in its stead was merely a flat-headed, reeded extension of the side jambs.

A door from Homewood, Baltimore. This house was completely rebuilt in 1801, using designs taken directly from the latest British Regency models.

From the 1830s onwards, too, glass – which in the context of the doorcase had hitherto been limited to the fanlight – began to appear in the actual body of the front door, so as to bring more natural light into the dark entrance hallways. In spite of what many modern 'period door' manufacturers are keen to suggest, glass rarely featured within the door during the entire Georgian era, although its use was not unknown in some rural regions, notably Northumberland; certainly glass was never employed in the now ubiquitous 'slipped fanlight' configuration so aggressively marketed by the purveyors of today's 'Georgian-style' front doors of varnished hardwood. Generally, only internal doors were found glazed – particularly those leading in and out of the kitchen, where the glass had an obvious practical benefit. In these instances, four or perhaps nine panes of glass would be inserted into the top half of the door. At the same time as the demise of the fanlight, however, householders began to remove the upper two panels of their front doors and insert in their place panes of plate glass, which was more able to withstand the stresses and tremors of daily door operation than its more fragile Georgian ancestors. This door glass was, like many of the window margin lights of the period, frequently stained, a development which laid the foundations for the sophisticated and colourful front-door compositions of the Victorian age.

As well as prompting progress in glass-making techniques, the Industrial Revolution also brought great improvements in the strength, malleability, lustre, and rapidity of manufacture of metal alloys. One immediate result was that brass, which in the years before the Regency period could only have been found adorning the doors and windows of the grandest houses, became considerably cheaper and more widely available during the early years of the nineteenth century. Casting techniques improved, too, and the simple cast-iron forms of the eighteenth century – when door furniture was fairly uncommon – were now transformed into lively and intricate designs. During the Regency the classic lion's-head door knocker became very popular, as did those incorporating such topical motifs as sphinxes, crocodiles, or naval emblems. For the more humble, rural dwelling, the classic Norfolk or Suffolk door latches were now adapted for mass-produced machine production. Bell-pushes started to appear in great numbers, too, invariably set in a circular brass surround at the side of the doorcase. In 1836 Charles Dickens, in his *Sketches by Boz*, described a walk to 'Eaton-square, then just building': 'What was our astonishment and indignation to find that bells were fast becoming the rule, and knockers the exception.'

Yet it must be remembered that the Regency door was not overburdened with door furniture. Letter boxes were, of course, a mid-Victorian innovation – the postal system only truly began in 1840 – while door numbers were only used sporadically during this period (although mandatory in London after 1805). Nor was the Regency door – in contrast to all the many modern 're-creations' – a backdrop for a panoply of shiny brass fittings. Although brass was more common than formerly, cast iron was still the most widely

Circular 'oeil de boeuf' and
semicircular 'lunette' windows
on the front elevation of
Jefferson's Monticello.

used material for door furniture. It was rarely left uncovered and was usually painted black to dull the surface; short-lived and messy 'Berlin black' was most frequently used, but modern blackboard paint is a good and more reliable substitute. A simple, black-painted knocker was probably what Dickens envisioned when he wrote *A Christmas Carol*; Marley's ghost would undoubtedly recoil in horror at some of the shiny fripperies now posing as 'Regency' or 'Victorian' reproductions. The unsubtle brightness and thin superficiality of many of these models – frequently in Britain of the lever-handled variety, which was rarely found on doors before the twentieth century – tend to obscure the aesthetic worth of the front doors to which they are attached. It is important, then, to retain all original knockers, hinges, locks, numbers, and other items of door furniture if you do have to repair or remove old doors; this applies as much to the simplest internal doors as to the grandest front entrances.

Door locks were also transformed during the Regency era, as the wealthy middle classes sought to give protection to the symbols of their new affluence. In some houses simple, functional rim locks in the Early Georgian fashion continued to be used; however, more security and aesthetically conscious households installed the new mortise locks – locks which operated within the fabric of the door, and had first appeared in the 1760s. Lock cases were now more often of stamped brass than of iron; particularly popular in this context was James Emerson's new, malleable brass of copper and zinc, patented in 1770. In 1784 Joseph Bramah invented the first door lock opened with a key which was not, as in the past, heavy and ponderous but small and easily pocketable. The lock itself was operated by the action of a rotating barrel, not via the traditional sliding bolt, an innovation further perfected in the 1840s in the form of the classic Yale cylindrical lock. In 1818 the Chubb lock was patented, a device whose mechanism was able to detect tiny variations in key patterns; this clearly allowed for far greater variety in the configuration of door keys and thus afforded far greater security. No longer were the front doors of Britain open to all comers: the Industrial Revolution now provided the wealthier sections of society with the luxury of protection from the thief, the mob, and the curious.

Today Regency doors are painted every conceivable colour, and are often – through a confusion of actual Georgian and Regency practice with the more recent Arts and Crafts and Modernist yearning for 'honest', revealed materials – stripped of their paintwork. Yet in Regency Britain doors, both internal and external, were always painted. They were only left bare if constructed of an expensive material such as seasoned oak or imported mahogany, in which case they would simply have been given repeated coats of beeswax. If merely made of pine or a similar softwood – as the vast majority of Regency doors were – front doors were painted a dark colour, while the door surround was painted broken white or 'stone colour'. Internal doors tended to reflect the colour scheme of the room or were painted in fashionable dark shades which matched the dark skirting – chocolate brown

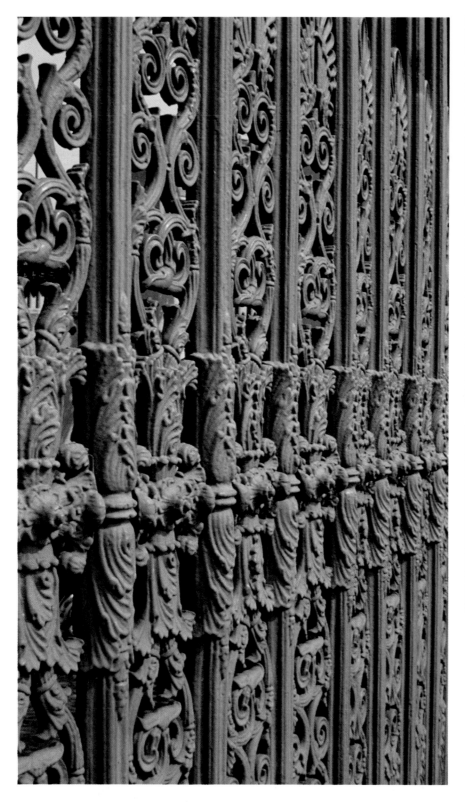

Regency railings painted green to suggest the patina of aged, antique bronze. From the Duke of Wellington's Apsley House at Hyde Park Corner in London.

Opposite: Nash's stuccoed Albany Terrace, Regent's Park, of the mid-1820s. Both the lampstands and the ironwork are Nash's own designs.

was a perennial favourite. External and particularly internal doors were often grained to imitate seasoned oak or other, more exotic woods – a traditional paint treatment which witnessed a great revival during the Regency.

Soane liked to paint his front doors green, in imitation of the weathered bronze apparently so prevalent in the ancient world. While this practice remained rather a personal taste, green was widely used to decorate railings adjacent to the front door, a practice which, again, seems to stem from the Neo-Classical predilection for a 'bronzed' effect. Nash, for example, specified that the railings outside his Regent's Park terraces should be painted 'the colour of bronze'. In this he followed Repton, who in 1803 had declared that: 'if we wish [painted ironwork] to resemble metal, and not appear of an inferior kind, a powdering of copper or gold dust on a green ground makes a bronze, and perhaps is the best colour for all ornamental rails of iron.'

Green was also the colour used to adorn the ironwork of newly fashionable verandahs and conservatories. In 1825 the paintmaker John Lingard was marketing his 'Immarcescible Bright Green' especially for this purpose. Blue, used for domestic metalwork of any pretension throughout the eighteenth century, had long since fallen out of favour; lead grey, though, was still widely employed for exterior ironwork of more modest character. Unfortunately, most green railings have been repainted since the Regency – usually in black, a fashion which only originated at the very end of the nineteenth century, or in the dark brown to which the original paint was left to fade. Some Regency ironwork has more recently been given back its green hue; it is, however, perhaps more important – especially in a terrace or street of relatively unified composition – to ensure that the colour of the exterior ironwork corresponds with that used on the adjacent houses, rather than to embark on the pursuit of complete historical authenticity.

Ironwork details from Nash's Regent's Park development of the 1820s.

Opposite: Gilded finials, such as this urn, were actually very rare during the Regency period – being largely confined to the palaces of the rich. Modern-day gold paint is never a very suitable substitute for real gilding in this or any other context.

WHEN I SAY WE SHALL LEAVE WYCOMBE ABBEY WEDNESDAY SENNIGHT I OUGHT TO ADD PROVIDED WE DO NOT SOME OF US OR ALL OF US BREAK OUR LIMBS OR OUR NECKS ON THESE HORRIBLY SLIPPERY BEAUTIFUL FLOORS AND STAIRS.

(MARIA EDGEWORTH, 1821)

The magnificent victories of Trafalgar and Waterloo; Britain's central role in shaping post-Napoleonic Europe and as the liberal conscience of the backward continental autocracies; her undeniable commercial and industrial pre-eminence – all these factors helped foster by 1820 a strong, oft-expressed preference for British products, habits, and values. Nowhere was this more clearly reflected than in the choice of materials to be used for the architectural detailing of the Regency home. British firms led the world in the manufacture of cast and wrought iron; thus, Regency designers and householders were correspondingly quick to embrace this versatile and revolutionary material. Nor were traditional materials exempted from this patriotic enthusiasm. In 1813 Rudolph Ackermann fulsomely lauded British marbles in a fittingly chauvinistic manner:

our native marbles are deserving public cultivation, and many of them approach to the perfection of the antiques . . . When we see men of rank and fortune interesting themselves in the adoption of marbles, the produce of their native country, we have cause to hope that they will obtain an universal interest and patronage.

This nationalistic fervour also extended to British wood. Foreign products such as mahogany, satinwood, rosewood, or even zebrawood – originating, like its namesake, from Africa, and similarly striped – were certainly much in demand for furniture of the period. For large areas of panelling and for other principal features of the interior, however, more familiar woods were generally used. For architectural elements, British oak or British or American deal (pine) were still greatly preferred. This bias in favour of home-grown or colonial woods was not merely a product of popular xenophobia but originated in financial necessity: the Napoleonic Wars, and particularly the post-1806 blockade, stifling imports of basic materials such as yellow Baltic deal, made it far more difficult to obtain foreign woods at an affordable price. Instead, native woods such as oak, pine,

A fireplace atlanta sumptuously smothered in gilt, at Lancaster House, London – erected after 1825 for George IV's brother the Duke of York. A succession of architects worked on the house: Robert Smirke, Benjamin Dean Wyatt, Philip Wyatt and (after 1838) Charles Barry.

Opposite: The staircase from Selwood Park, in Mitchell's view of 1801. The iron balusters are in the form of lyres – a very common motif of the last quarter of the eighteenth century.

Regency plasterwork details from an interior by Busby in Hove, Sussex. Anthemions, acanthus leaves and Soane's 'British' order (complete with daffodil in the centre of the capital) are all evident.

and – enjoying a new vogue – elm were widely promoted. Ackermann particularly recommended employing good old British oak for newly fashionable Gothic interiors.

The best oak panelling was left unpainted, so guests would not fail to appreciate the enormity of the house owner's taste, wealth, and patriotism. In richer households, Jamaican or Brazilian mahogany was equally treasured and prominently displayed. Patriotically permissible on account of its British colonial or allied origin, waxed mahogany remained popular for doors, furniture, stair handrails, and, for those who could afford it, large expanses of wall panelling throughout the Regency period. Any woods aside from expensive oak, mahogany, or other exotica were, however, inevitably painted – either a flat colour or grained in imitation of these more sophisticated woods – or papered. This served both to hide the irregularities in their grain – which some modern house owners are so keen to expose – and to conceal their true (cheap) identity.

Oak was still popular for floorboards. Again, though, most households had to make do with inferior woods, which were usually partly or wholly covered to hide their raw, knotty surfaces. There were no particular rules as to the dimensions of floorboards; nor were the boards necessarily of a consistent size within a single floor. Patent machines to plane timber uniformly were introduced during the 1790s, but it was not until the 1830s that identical boards were produced by steam-powered, mechanical saws. The popularity of fitted carpets made the elaborately designed wooden floor less of a necessity – a development noted by Sheraton, who famously remarked that 'since the introduction of carpets, fitted all over the floor of a room, the nicety of flooring anciently practised in the best houses, is now laid aside'.

Floorboards were often nailed at their edges, at an angle of 45 degrees, and the joint subsequently concealed by the next board. In 1803 Sheraton summarized the most common methods for laying wooden floors: 'There are three methods by which floors are laid. First, with plain jointed edges, and nailed down. Second, jointing and ploughing the edges to receive a wainscot tongue about an inch broad, and a bare quarter thick . . . Third, when they are laid with douwells of oak-board into the edge.' Not long after this account appeared metal plates, rather than dowels, began to be inserted into the grooving in adjacent boards, so as to ensure an even firmer joint. And by 1833 Loudon was recommending thicker boards, 'sometimes . . . three inches thick', to give added strength and 'to lessen the risk of their being burnt through by fire'.

In 1780 single-joisted floors (with the joists all running in the same direction), supported by large structural timbers, were still very much the rule for the average house. The joists ran from front to back, bearing on the external and (if they existed) party walls and possibly on the central spine wall, too. This simple method of construction allowed the large, structural beams to spread the weight of the spine wall down the centre of the house, with its doors, doorcases, and stairs, to the outer shell and also allowed floors

Grained pine panelling in a Jacobean Revival style from Temple Newsam House, Leeds.

Opposite: The grained wooden chimneypiece from the Great Hall at Temple Newsam – as redecorated in the late 1820s. At the same time that the graining was applied, the surrounding plasterwork was painted to resemble ashlar blocks.

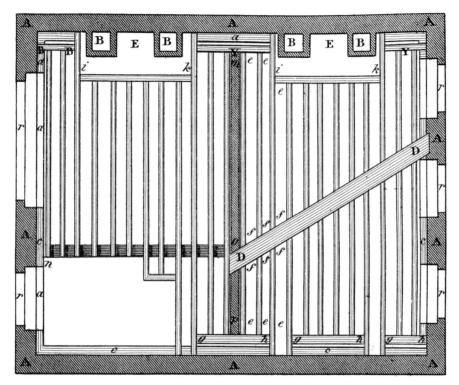

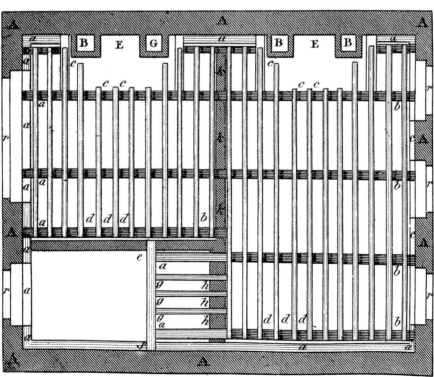

Timber floor construction as
demonstrated by Peter
Nicholson in his 1812 manual.

Opposite: An impressive parquet
floor design from the Parlour at
Monticello.

and ceilings above the ground floor to be wholly self-supporting. If there were greater loading requirements then additional, transverse joists and beams could be added – though not with any precise knowledge of the exact effect this would have: it was only in 1840 that the first guide to gauging joist thicknesses for specific spans was published. However, the upper floors of most Regency houses did not need to bear enormous weights, as most entertaining was done on the ground floor and not the first, as had often been the case earlier in the Georgian era. The concept of the 'rustic' ground floor of services and servant accommodation, with incoming guests proceeding directly to the principal rooms on the floor above, was now very outdated.

Timber floors were, in common with stone examples, sometimes limewashed. (This valuable protective coating is still widely available and allows floors and walls to 'breathe' – that is, permits moisture to pass in and out of the underlying material rather than causing it to be trapped inside, prompting damp problems.) The visual effect of limewashing wooden boards was to produce an attractive silvery sheen, of the type modern 'limed' furniture tries to recapture. In 1772 an American visitor noted that English deal floors 'are washed and rubbed almost daily' with limewater, resulting in 'a whitish appearance, and an air of freshness and cleanliness'. (In America limewater was also used, but American households tended to rely much more on good old soap-and-water scrubbing or sweeping the floor with flowers.) A similar, white patina was achieved through the widespread practice of cleaning wooden floors by scrubbing them with dry sand, sometimes mixed with fresh herbs. Alternatively, aromatic herbs such as mint or tansy could be rubbed into the grain to give the boards both a fresh odour and a slightly darker stain.

If the floorboards were not made of seasoned oak or other expensive wood, they were always covered in some fashion. As with clay or plaster floors, a common practice was to paint them to resemble marble blocks. At the same time, a terracotta paint – often finished with a yellow glaze or with limewash – was also widely used, an effect which, interestingly, recalled the traditional, modest, clay floor. By the 1820s the stencilling of floorboards, long popular in the United States but previously never very fashionable in Britain, was also enjoying a vogue, while parquetry was back in fashion – not for whole floors, but for the newly popular borders being left around the carpets. This in turn prompted a wholesale revival of parquetry – at least in the larger homes – by the end of the period: in 1837, the year that Victoria ascended the throne, craftsman and writer Peter Nicholson was writing that 'The fashion for laying floors with various coloured woods, disposed in patterns, seems now to become more general in this country'.

Wood was not, of course, the only material used for Regency floors. Floors varied as much as did the levels of wealth and pretension. More basic homes, especially in rural areas, were still given 'stuccoed' or clay floors. The 'stucco' floors of cottages and outbuildings were made from a basic plaster

One of Mary Ellen Best's marvellous York cottage interiors, painted in 1836. Best's pictures tell us much about the average home of the period; this view shows reddened, tessellated brick paviors on the floor.

recipe, which usually included a natural pigment – most often pig's blood –
to give the dried 'stucco' a brown colour. In common with so many surfaces
of the Regency era, these floors were often disguised as something else:
painted to resemble black and white marble squares, or simply covered with a
layer of whitewash or limewash. In 1814 P. F. Tingry's *Painter's and
Varnisher's Guide* noted that: 'Some floors have been executed of plaster, on
which the lemon yellow colour destined for *parquets* of oak produces a very
good effect.' Alas, clay or stucco floors rarely survive: either the surfaces have
broken up through constant wear, or social aspirations have prompted their
replacement by more sophisticated wood or stone alternatives. It is
interesting to note that, at the other end of the social scale, floors in scagliola
– a plaster compound outlined below – were also denoted by the name
'stucco'. The vast amounts of money laid out on such rare and colourful
treatments, however, were usually wasted: ironically, scagliola floors proved
even more fragile than their distant, humbler cousins.

For those who could afford it – or for those who lived near a suitable
quarry – solid floors still represented the acme of taste. The classic solid
floor was still much as it had been during the preceding century: large slabs
of Portland or similarly pale-coloured stone interset with tiny diamonds of
dark grey slate or marble, or perhaps variations on the theme of black and
white marble squares. This type of heavy flooring was most prevalent in
ground-floor hallways, both to impress visitors and to bear the constant
weight of social assemblies.

For the poorer households random flags – possibly decorated for special
occasions with renewable patterns in chalk or soot – or even tessellated brick
paviours, reddened with pigments based on animal blood, had to suffice.
Loudon's *Encyclopaedia* of 1833 featured thirteen different designs for paving
in coloured bricks. Coloured tiles, however, were more of a Victorian fad:
although used in grand halls of the 1830s, the production of more
sophisticated, hard-wearing tiles – often with indented patterns filled with
slip – did not really take off until the 1840s.

Like so many other elements of the Regency house, the panelling and
plasterwork of the period were actually simpler and more austere, and not
more elaborate, than had been the case in previous decades. This was not,
of course, true of every home. The more daring and innovative interiors of
Britain's grand mansions, or indeed of the homes of architects such as Hope
or Soane, included designs and motifs that were heavily influenced by the
latest developments in France or Germany or the latest archaeological
discoveries in Italy or Greece. However, it is dangerous to take such grand,
ambitious decorative solutions as the model for the average home of the
period. Most Regency walls and ceilings of relatively modest dimensions
tended to follow Ackermann's dictum that a 'simple and chaste character
is best'.

This was particularly true of mouldings – now far more restrained in
form and use than those of the ages of Kent or Adam. Their reticence

*Typical plaster detailing of the
Regency period, drawing both
on the latest Regency motifs and
on traditional Palladian forms.*

Plain Regency fireplace and restrained mouldings, relieved only by a simple Grecian frieze, in the Governor's Room at Soane's Bank of England. Soane's work here is now mostly destroyed or altered.

Below: Characteristic Soaneian arches with reeded soffits – a common decorative feature of the period – in the Bank of England's (now demolished) Corporation and Colonial Office. A rare photographic view of 1894.

*Detail of a fireplace from
Homewood, Baltimore.
Fireplaces such as this could be
provided with an inset of
marble or scagliola.*

allowed the colourful ensembles of window drapery, paint, wallpaper, and furniture – and not, as had been the case with most Palladian interiors, the cornice, doorcase, or dado – to provide the principal visual interest within the room. This is not to say that the vocabulary of Regency joiners and plasterers became more limited. Quite the reverse: recently rediscovered Greek and Roman patterns, Gothic forms of an academic authenticity markedly different from the fripperies of Batty Langley and his followers, and even so-called Egyptian motifs were juxtaposed with the standard Palladian forms of the mid-eighteenth century.

The resultant compositions were, however, delicate and mostly of low relief, contrasting sharply with the heavier, traditional mouldings such as the ubiquitous egg-and-dart (although the simple, heavy ovolo remained popular in America for door and window mouldings for many years). Grecian motifs were naturally very popular, particularly the anthemion or the continuous and Vitruvian scrolls, used by Holland and later by Soane to decorate pilasters and the soffits of arches. Topical, political motifs were also widely used – notably, after 1811, the Prince Regent's three feathers. Such motifs were often extended to the ceiling edge, although the rest of the ceiling itself usually remained unadorned. While friezes were increasingly left bare and cornices were being constricted in width, low-relief decoration was, by 1800, being applied for the first time to ceiling borders, a trend which continued throughout the nineteenth century.

Reflecting the restraint and simplicity of Regency joinery and plasterwork was the most common moulding of the period, the humble bead. When used in a linked combination of two or more beads, the outermost edges of which were usually flush with the adjacent fillet or surface, the moulding was termed 'reeding'. One of the best source-books for Regency mouldings, Peter Nicholson's *Mechanical Exercises* of 1812, abounds with beads and reeding. Reeding was applied to cornices, chimneypieces, door surrounds, dados, and skirting; there were even 'reeded' glazing bars, set with two or three deeply undercut, 'quirked' beads. Quirking was a Greek device used to obtain a greater sense of depth and play of shadows from a basically low-relief moulding or surface and was very prevalent in the Regency house. Deeply quirked single beads were often found placed between wall panels, framing niches, or inserted into the middle of single doors to give the false impression of a double-doored entrance.

The more important a room, of course, the heavier and more profuse the carved or moulded ornamentation was. However, even the grandest rooms were designed primarily as showcases for furniture and coverings, and not to display the work of the carver or joiner.

Whereas the cornice, skirting, and dado were increasingly restrained, plaster was still used to create additional visual interest on Regency walls. Regency designers and craftsmen continued Robert Adam's practice of inserting circular medallions or rectangular panels, set with suitably Neo-Classical motifs, into the wall space. The form of the plaster and the

techniques used for its application differed little from previous practice.
Internal plasters continued to be made using a base of lime or gypsum; the
latter (popularly known as plaster of Paris) was the most favoured owing to
its faster setting time. This basic material was then mixed with animal hair,
or possibly with straw or reeds, to make a more durable and more binding
substance. The resultant plaster was then applied in three or more coats over
laths generally made from deal, fir, beech, or inferior oak. From the early
nineteenth century, plaster was additionally strengthened by the provision of
wire netting stapled or tacked to joists, a technique patented in 1797.
'Martin's Cement', patented in 1834, was a branded gypsum plaster which
used pearl ash and a small amount of sulphuric acid to produce a tougher
plaster.

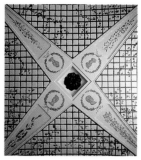

*Right: John Soane and his wife
breakfasting in what is now,
predictably, called the Breakfast
Room at 12 Lincoln's Inn
Fields, in a watercolour by
J. M. Gandy of 1796. The
'starfish' ceiling design (shown,
above, as it is today) is Soane's;
the painted decoration is by
John Crace. No. 12 was
Soane's first home in the
square; in 1812 he moved next
door to the specially remodelled
no.13, which now houses the
splendid museum.*

Inside the grander houses individual ornaments of gypsum plaster were
executed in place. In the majority of homes, however, premoulded ornament,
prefabricated in workshops and then fixed on site, was the rule. This was
fixed onto the third coat of plaster by means of liquid slip and sometimes
re-pressed when in position to give greater definition. Straight cornices and
dado rails were usually applied using a specially shaped tool, confusingly
called a 'horse'.

In the more pretentious houses, too, plaster decoration was frequently
picked out in gilt – often to excess. The displays of gold in the sumptuous
interiors of Brighton Pavilion or Lancaster House were deliberately designed
to achieve a stunning – if vulgar – effect. In the Pavilion's Music Room
Frederick Crace, who employed thirty-four assistants to work on this room
alone, directed that four different types of gilding – each a slight shade of
red, green, or white, according to which tiny quantity of appropriately
coloured metal had been added to the gold – be used on the ceiling. As
historian John Morley has noted: 'The total effect is somewhat like that of
a great lacquer box.' Most of the population could not, of course, afford to
indulge in the gilt fantasies of George IV or his brother the Duke of York.
But where they could, they picked out their plaster cornices in gilt or rapidly
tarnishing gold paint. They never, though, attempted to pick out mouldings
in contrasting shades of paint; this is a somewhat unhappy invention of
recent times.

Not all paint or gilding concealed real plaster. The Regency witnessed a
vast increase in popularity of that versatile, waterproof, and peculiarly British
material, papier mâché. The term was first employed by the French
Huguenot artisans working in east London in the early eighteenth century.
By 1800 the manufacturing base for papier mâché had moved from
Spitalfields to Wolverhampton, and the quality and durability had improved
substantially. Henry Clay's 1772 patent specified a product made from rag
paper pasted together, dried on a stove, soaked in oil, and then, if a long
length was required, wrapped around greased planks of wood. The finished
product, painted white or another appropriate colour, or gilded, was much
used for complex wall and ceiling decoration. It was also very popular for

Opposite: This detail of the richly-gilded plasterwork of Lancaster House shows how important mirrors were in the planning of the Regency interior. The architectural use of mirrors in place of plastered or panelled surfaces was a fashion partly popularized by Sir John Soane.

A splendid ceiling from Lancaster House.

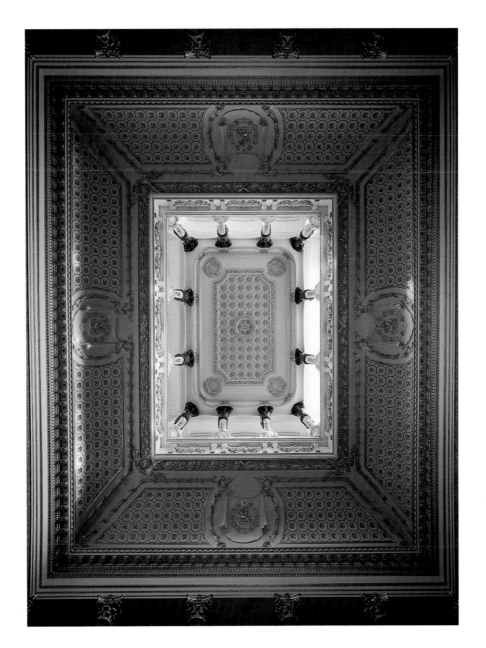

A scagliola pilaster and column from a house of 1830 in Clifton, Bristol.

*Not scagliola but marbled wood;
the marbling being applied to a
pilaster of 1837.*

mirror and picture frames, when it was either gilded or 'japanned' with black
lacquer. By 1830 it was – together with its superior French relative, carton
pierre, made from pulped paper, glue, and whiting – much sought after as a
lighter, hard-wearing substitute for wood in furniture and household objects
of all kinds. In 1827 decorator Nathaniel Whittock wrote that such
ornaments 'have a beautiful effect on painted ceilings, gilt capitals of columns
&c; and the intelligent decorator will see that any clever boy may produce
them'.

Papier mâché was by no means the only deceptive material used on the
walls of Regency homes. Regency householders delighted in using finishes or
substances which were not what they seemed, which mimicked costly
materials only to be seen in profusion in the great houses of the country.
One of the most successful of these Regency illusions was scagliola: made
from pigmented plaster and marble chips (or a similar aggregate) cast and
then polished, it could be fashioned to resemble any species of true marble.
Another variation on this method, marezzo marble, used only plaster.

By 1820 the fashion for scagliola had spread like wildfire. It was made
into wall panels, where it was often varnished or polished with linseed oil,
finishes which have not improved the colour or, given scagliola's
susceptibility to damp, the durability of the wall surface over the years. The
end result could be hugely impressive: on the staircase at Charles Barry's
Reform Club in London, for instance, a sumptuous effect of richly coloured
marbles was achieved in the late 1830s at a fraction of the cost of the real
thing. Scagliola was also used to form substitute marble columns or pilasters
and sham marble table tops. And as already noted, it was used to mimic
marble floors – where it was able to match marble's colour and grain, but
never its durability. One solution was to use scagliola flooring only for the
newly fashionable carpet borders. 'In some cases', advised Loudon, 'the
preferable mode is . . . to finish the margin [of the floor] with scagliola, and
cover the interior with carpeting.' Wherever marble might be used, but was
either too expensive or would prove too great a weight for the supporting
structure to bear, scagliola could be substituted.

A further use for scagliola was in facing the side supports and the
mantelshelves of fireplaces. The Regency chimneypiece, like other interior
architectural features, was simpler and more reticent than its Palladian and
Baroque predecessors – and indeed than its more elaborate French
contemporaries. It still followed the basic format of the Palladian
chimneypiece, which in turn was derived from Elizabethan and Jacobean
precedents: a projecting entablature was supported by consoles, themselves
carried by two simple columns or pilasters. Regency examples, though, had
become excessively plain, with little superimposed decoration; all you would
find might be two small paterae inserted, one at each corner, in the inside
slip (the internal frame). Architectural elements, and not surface decoration,
were now accorded the prime role in the composition.

Except in the homes of the richest families, Regency chimneypieces

Opposite: A colourful and decidedly eccentric fireplace design of 1810 by Landi.

Right: A beautifully balanced composition of a delicate fireplace framed by two large alcoves by the prolific and highly successful architect James Wyatt.

Below: 'Jacobethan' chimneypieces of the late Regency period, with prominent tiled insets.

rarely varied from this standard, rectilinear form. Supporting pilasters were, for example, rarely tapered, and attendant caryatids or terms were devices which only guarded the fires of the wealthy. Most often the only profusely applied decoration was recessed reeding; the visual result was still a far more two-dimensional composition than those designed by Kent, Adam, or Chambers. Even the luxurious Chinese Room at Temple Newsam of 1827, for example, was, in marked contrast to its lively Chinese wallpaper, provided with an extremely plain fireplace, with few mouldings and a bare central tablet – in Adam's day the decorative centrepiece.

This type of small, simple fireplace was ubiquitous in British homes during the late Regency period. This one is from an upper floor of a house by Busby in Hove, Sussex.

Such austerity won wide acclaim from those of a more puritanical bent. Out went scantily clad caryatids; instead, the Regency chimneypiece realized William Chambers's prudish precept that 'All nudities and indecent representations must be avoided, both in chimneypieces and in every other ornament of apartments to which children, ladies, and other modest, grave persons, have constant recourse.'

With the spread of Gothic fashion in the 1820s, however, decorative licence was back in fashion. Thus, while Ackermann's Classical chimneypieces remained excessively plain, his featured Gothic examples were covered with low-relief yet vigorous embellishment, usually based on those ubiquitous motifs, the quatrefoil and the crocket. Representational decoration of a highly frivolous (though suitably antique) nature – even including a diaphanously clad maiden or two – was permitted on 'Egyptian' fireplaces, although the basic architectural form still rarely departed from the trusted formula of two pillars and a shelf.

The design of Regency fireplaces was also affected by technological improvements. Seventeenth- and eighteenth-century examples had for the most part been too large to function efficiently. The invention of the Rumford stove in 1796 – detailed in the chapter below – engendered a revolution in attitudes to the arrangement of the fireplace, as householders recognized the need for more precisely controlled grates and for smaller fireplace openings. Thus, the Regency fireplace became not only increasingly simple, but also increasingly small.

Paradoxically, however, the fireplace was more than ever the focus of the room. From the 1780s onwards furniture began to be moved more informally around the rooms and, given the nature of the British climate, naturally gravitated towards the fire. Ackermann held that the resultant heightened prominence of the fireplace in the principal rooms of the house was a peculiarly British solution; the corresponding effect, he asserted, was a healthier household and a healthier nation.

The position of the fireplace was governed largely by the function, not the appearance, of a room. Thus, while the principal rooms retained centrally disposed chimneypieces, it was still wholly possible to match the chimneypiece's size to its environment, closely following Hope's sound dictum that 'the size of the chimney must depend on the dimensions of the room wherein it is placed'. (Alas, this basic common sense is often forgotten

Above: Chimneypieces from Homewood, Baltimore.

Right: Detail of a typically reticent and architectural fireplace from the Library at Sir John Soane's Museum, Lincoln's Inn, London. The only decoration Soane allows is the reeding and the small paterae inserted at the edge of the mantelshelf.

The fireplace from the Small Drawing Room at Thomas Hope's Surrey home of Deepdene, shown in a watercolour of 1823. The fireplace is of green Mona marble from Anglesey, while the fire tongs have been formally arranged on the grate; in front is a fashionable hearthrug.

Opposite: A cantilevered iron staircase at Pitshanger Manor, Ealing, west London.

by today's purchasers of over-elaborate and over-sized salvaged fireplaces.)

Although simpler in appearance, the Regency fireplace was constructed from a far broader range of materials than its predecessors. White marble was no longer the most popular material, as it had been in the days of Adam. As already seen, coloured scagliola was often employed, as were unusually coloured native marbles. Ackermann was a particular devotee of the sage-green Mona marble from Anglesey in Wales: in 1816 he eulogized 'the importance of this invaluable marble to the purposes of interior decoration', arguing that, 'it vies in richness of colour with the precious marbles of antiquity, and affords to the artist, at a reasonable price, a means for . . . splendid decoration'. Once again, decorative innovation and national chauvinism were united in an uncertain alliance.

Grander marble or stone chimneypieces were also provided with applied ornamentation in ormolu or bronze. Neither of these treatments were quite what they seemed to be at first glance: 'bronze' was usually only bronze powder on a painted base of green or brown, while 'ormolu' was not, in most houses, true gilded bronze, but a cheaper variant – lacquered brass. This 'English ormolu' was also applied copiously to the frames of the overmantel. During the Regency the overmantel, too, was of a decidedly architectural form, generally either comprising three horizontal mirrors or one large upright, both often topped with an entablature. More exotic decorative finishes were also used on this feature – which, after all, was the visual focus of the room. Verre églomisé – engraved gilt under a protective glass surface – and numerous forms of lacquering were all utilized to give a more brilliant finish.

Verre églomisé and expensive marbles were not, of course, within reach of the average householder. Chimneypieces made from, and decorated with, far humbler materials were the rule in these homes. Cast-iron fireplaces were very prevalent by 1840, often blacked and perhaps with patterned tiles stuck directly onto the splayed frames. The decorative opportunities of the fireplace tile were not fully exploited until the 1850s; however, another ceramic *was* widely used for Regency chimneypieces. By 1800 the Coade factory was marketing a range of Coade stone chimneypieces, which ranged in price from an astonishingly cheap 25 shillings each to a by no means ruinous 14 guineas.

By far the commonest materials for cheaper fireplaces, however, were plaster and pine. Simple 'Greek' pine fireplaces were being offered by Chippendale, Haig and Co. for £1 19s. by the 1780s, while their plaster equivalents could be had for between £1 and £6 each. In 1833 Loudon reported that plaster chimneypieces were selling in London for 7 shillings, with reeded ones at 28 shillings. Pine examples were invariably painted – usually a broken white (as specified by Chippendale himself) – and were never left bare, nor subsequently stripped.

Owing to the dangers of warping through heat, exotic woods were rarely employed around the fireplace. Instead, the showcase for woods such as

A simple iron stair of the 1820s, designed by the great architect C. R. Cockerell.

Right: Iron balusters of the 1830s from a house in Bath.

Opposite: The iron-and-stone staircase from Sir John Soane's Museum in Lincoln's Inn Fields. Note the marbling on the walls and the red and yellow stair carpet – a recent recreation of what was there in Soane's day.

mahogany was the staircase, where it could be sparingly used for handrails and balusters to convey an impression of warmth and taste – and wealth. The staircase was often one of the most impressive and graceful features of the Regency interior. Cast- or wrought-iron balusters became increasingly common – unembellished and unadorned, or interspersed with delicate panels featuring characteristically Greek motifs such as the acanthus or the anthemion. In these instances only the mahogany, oak, or grained pine handrail remained as a reminder of the traditional wooden stair. Even the treads and risers could be of iron. And bulky wooden newel posts were often replaced with an S-shaped termination of thinner iron balusters – a particularly common motif in houses of all kinds in the 1820s and 1830s.

The most remarkable property of the Regency staircase, and indeed of the Regency interior as a whole, was its lack of apparent structural support, consequent on the development of the iron frame and the cantilever. Regency designers delighted in using iron to enable staircases of great grace and delicacy, with dramatically swooping and curving handrails, to be placed in improbable situations. How, observers wondered, did they stay up? The more ostentatious designers dispensed with the soffits under the stairs altogether, creating the impression of an open-string staircase that appeared to be made merely of treads and risers piled up on top of one another in mid-air. By the 1820s the most radically planned houses were not even bothering to hide the ingenious iron supports. At Sezincote, for example, the iron girders which carried the main stair were left totally bare and pierced in a vaguely decorative way. This solution was subsequently widely used by architects such as George Gilbert Scott; yet it was not, perhaps, a development really typical of the Regency. The latter was, after all, a period in which illusion and good-natured deception were combined in a more self-mocking and gently humorous way – attitudes which surely contrast strongly with the earnestness and moral rectitude of the Victorians.

The Regency staircase from The Argory, County Armagh, Northern Ireland. Note the marbled walls and the lack of any apparent support for the stair treads, which ascend with a breathtaking freedom.

IT IS PITIFUL TO SUBMIT TO FARTHING CANDLE EXISTENCE WHEN SCIENCE PUTS SUCH INTENSE GRATIFICATION WITHIN YOUR REACH. DEAR LADY, SPEND ALL YOUR FORTUNE ON A GAS APPARATUS.

(SYDNEY SMITH, 1821)

Mary Ellen Best's watercolour of the kitchen at Elmswell Hall, York, of 1834. The small rug on the paved floor and the large dresser, bedecked with crockery and kitchen utensils, were typical features of Regency kitchens.

Before the end of the eighteenth century, most Georgian interiors were dark and gloomy. After sunset the only illumination available to most people was either a dim, unreliable oil lamp or erratic, guttering, mutton-smelling tallow candles; beeswax candles were available, but only for the rich. Outside the home, provision for night-time lighting was little better. London and the more prosperous cities had oil lamps hanging from green-painted stands placed along the major thoroughfares; however, in the days before gas, they were often more trouble than they were worth.

By 1840, however, the methods of lighting both house interiors and town and village streets had undergone a dramatic revolution – a series of developments which profoundly influenced the way interiors were disposed and decorated and the manner in which indoor and outdoor activities were planned. The first major breakthrough was the invention of the Argand lamp. In 1783 the Swiss chemist François Ami Argand patented a new form of lamp, also known in Britain as a colza-oil lamp after the thick, greenish-yellow rape-seed oil it burned. Argand's lamp was constructed around a revolutionary new circular cotton wick with an internal air channel and a larger surface area from which to burn the oil. The wick itself was placed in a funnel (originally of iron, later of glass) to help promote the upward flow of air. A further distinctive element was the oil reservoir, installed half-way up the side of the funnel so the thick oil could flow to the bottom of the wick.

Argand lamps were relatively common by 1810; by 1820 they had appeared in engravings of interiors in Ackermann's *Repository* and Pyne's *Royal Residences*. As art historian Elspeth Moncrieff has remarked: 'Suddenly a light was available which produced ten to twelve times the light of a single candle, transforming the activities which could be carried out after darkness.' Among the more respectable of these activities was the use of the new sofa-

A colza-oil lamp provides the only light source in this 1830s self-portrait by the Irish artist Daniel Maclise.

Opposite: An impressive array of grand chandeliers in Pellatt and Green's shop in St Paul's Churchyard, London, in a view by Ackermann. Such confections were, alas, affordable only by the wealthy few.

tables as a central base for reading, writing, needlework, and such occupations. Altogether, the difference in the levels of illumination was astounding – so marked, in fact, that some observers readily attributed women's nervous disorders to the unnatural brightness of the new lamps.

Argand lamps were made from a variety of materials – an observer of 1786 noted 'crystal, lacquer and metal ones, silver and brass and every possible shade' – and, while primarily a utilitarian element, they were very much in keeping with the style of the age. Often incorporating Greek or Gothic motifs, the best were executed in Sheffield plate, others in brass, bronze or ormolu. They could be many-branched, and indeed could metamorphose into full-blooded (if not extremely graceful) chandeliers. In 1809 the 'sinumbra' lamp solved the problem of the bulky, shadow-casting reservoir, which was such a rebuke to the decorated elegance of the stem. Yet although passing the oil through tubes in the rim of the lampshade enabled the reservoir to be removed, there was still the problem presented by the very nature of the thick, viscous colza-oil itself – effectively a block to any truly light, graceful, and unobtrusive lamp design. Whale oil was promoted by optimistic entrepreneurs, but proved almost as sluggish as colza-oil; in the event it was not until the 1860s that an effective, more refined substitute – paraffin – was found for colza. In the 1790s the Frenchman Carcel invented a clockwork mechanism to pump the oil into the wick, yet this device was by no means cheap, and anyway production was soon halted as the factory was overcome by the tide of revolution. Thirty years later another Frenchman, Franchot, pioneered an ingenious spring-loaded piston to achieve the same end; his lamps were soon known as 'moderateurs', after the name of the valve needed to control the oil flow.

All of these variations, however, were relatively expensive. Many houses continued to rely on good old candlepower for their internal illumination (and Christine Edzard's excellent film of *Little Dorrit* reveals just how little light these candles imparted to the gloomy interiors of the period). The characteristic Regency candlestick epitomized, perhaps more than any other single item, the exquisite taste and craftsmanship of the period. As executed by Paul Storr or other leading silversmiths of the day, it was a strong and distinctly architectural composition, with clean lines and minimal detail. The most popular form was a fluted stick, perhaps with a Corinthian capital and a pyramidal or domed foot.

There was also that exotic invention, the telescopic candlestick – patented in 1796 and highly sought after for the next thirty years. Tripod candlesticks, too, were much in vogue. So, for those who could afford them, were elaborate chandeliers; with sinuous, sweeping arms, reflective ormolu frames, and many-faceted cut-glass drops, the chandelier remained one of the principal status symbols of the pretentious Regency home.

Twenty years after the Argand lamp first appeared, a new and even more astounding technological wonder brightened Regency homes and streets still further. In 1787 Lord Dundonald installed coal-gas lighting in his home, and

Lamplighters and a very early,
green-painted street gas lamp.
From W. H. Pyne's The
Costume of Great Britain *of*
1805.

'A peep at the gas lights in Pall Mall.' A cartoon of 1809 poking fun at the recent revolutionary introduction of public gas lighting in London's streets.

in 1803 another industrious immigrant, the extrovert Anglicized Moravian Frederick Winsor, erected the first public gas lights in Westminster's Pall Mall – additionally fitting up his own house with one-and-a-half-inch gas pipes in the process. Winsor subsequently shot to prominence, and earned the wide-eyed admiration of the Prince Regent (always something of a small boy at heart), by spectacularly illuminating the façade of Carlton House with gaslight for the King's birthday. Encouraged by the Prince, in 1812 he founded the Gas-Light and Coke Company at Cannon Row in Westminster, and from there he pumped gas to light such prominent edifices as Westminster Bridge and the Drury Lane Theatre. Two years later additional gasworks were opened in Shoreditch, Spitalfields, and Finsbury, and by the mid-1820s Winsor was supplying 70,000 lamps (for private homes and over 215 miles of streets) in the capital. Gaslight became a permanent fixture; in 1823 even the romantic novelist Walter Scott, whose books were far removed from the exigencies of modern industrial life, installed gas lighting at his house in Abbotsford.

The pace of progress did not instantly solve every lighting problem. The brightness of the gas lamps could not be increased; thus there simply had to be more of them. More seriously, the new gas piping inside the home was often carelessly buried under only a thin layer of plaster, or sited adjacent to heat sources or main passageways. Many gas explosions occurred during the

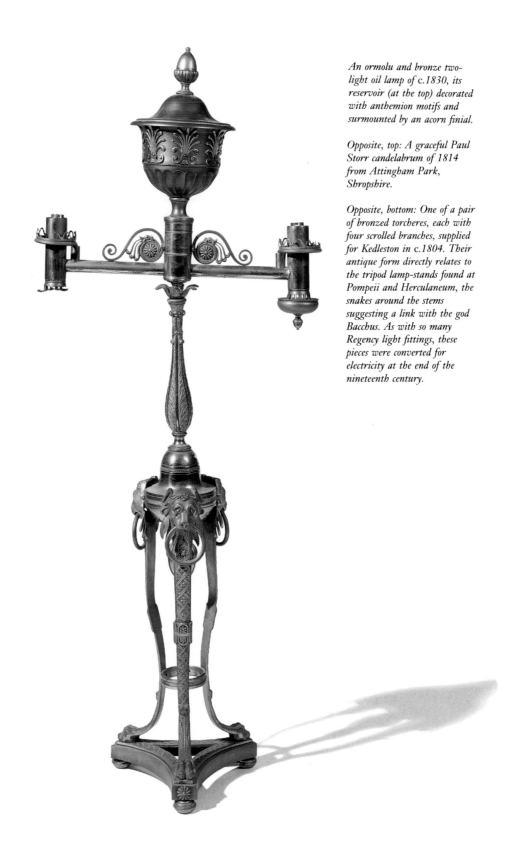

An ormolu and bronze two-light oil lamp of c.1830, its reservoir (at the top) decorated with anthemion motifs and surmounted by an acorn finial.

Opposite, top: A graceful Paul Storr candelabrum of 1814 from Attingham Park, Shropshire.

Opposite, bottom: One of a pair of bronzed torcheres, each with four scrolled branches, supplied for Kedleston in c.1804. Their antique form directly relates to the tripod lamp-stands found at Pompeii and Herculaneum, the snakes around the stems suggesting a link with the god Bacchus. As with so many Regency light fittings, these pieces were converted for electricity at the end of the nineteenth century.

1820s and 1830s, serving to demonstrate the fragility and jerry-building of some of the new speculative terraces by neatly blowing off entire front façades. Nevertheless, gas lights were a vast improvement on both candlelight and oil lamps. Never again would families have to curtail their reading or sewing at dusk; no longer would the pedestrian have to endure the type of horrific street conditions recorded by contemporary observers.

Unfortunately, both gas lights and colza-oil lamps are now extremely hard to find. The spread of electricity some decades later saw most of the stylish Regency light fittings heavily adapted, wholly replaced, or simply crudely ripped out. Thankfully, this has not been the fate of kitchen appliances; many of the stoves and ranges of the period still survive in private homes, as well as in museums. By 1790 the hob grate – a basket flanked with flat-topped hobs, designed to keep kettles and pots warm – had become hugely popular, and original or reproduction examples of these can still be widely found. The hob grate was not, like earlier versions, freestanding but set into the fireplace and was commercially available in three basic patterns: 'Bath', 'Pantheon', and 'Forest', each distinguished by the form of the central plate linking the two hobs. A further improvement was the provision of movable iron plates to regulate the size of the chimney opening, to create what became known as a 'register grate'. Even registers, though, were still smoky and inefficient, with much of the heat disappearing up the chimney flue. By 1810, however, the situation had changed markedly: new, heat-efficient grates were all the rage, and as chimneypieces became simpler in design, the technology of the grate was becoming ever more complex.

The progenitor of the fireplace revolution was the colourful figure Benjamin Thompson, an American adventurer and amateur engineer who was awarded the improbable title of Count Rumford by an enraptured Elector of Bavaria in 1784. As Southey noted in 1807, Rumford was 'a philosopher, the first person who has applied scientific discoveries to the ordinary purposes of life'. During a visit to England, Rumford was appalled by the primitive condition of the fireplaces he saw, in which most of the heat went up the chimney and most of the smoke into the room. The practical result of his concern was the essay 'Chimney Fireplaces' of 1796. This comprised a number of recommendations: a constricted flue throat, to confine the fire to the grate and also to create enough low pressure to promote an upward draught; a smoke shelf to be placed behind the throat, to stop rain and soot falling back down the chimney; a smaller opening for the fireplace as a whole; and angled grate backs and sides, made not of iron (as had been used for hob and register grates) but of a non-conducting material such as firebricks, which would reflect the heat forward into the room.

The effect of Rumford's treatise was instantaneous. New, cast-iron 'Rumford' grates were soon being manufactured, while many existing fireplaces were modified to fit many of the Count's specifications. Not all his suggestions were immediately taken up, though: the use of firebricks in place of the much-loved iron fireback did not catch on until mid-century. In 1800

Opposite: Count Rumford and his great invention immortalized in a contemporary print.

Right: An iron grate by Carron and Company c.1823 from Marble Hill House, Twickenham, Middlesex.

Below: Chimneypieces from London's *Suburban Gardener of 1838.*

 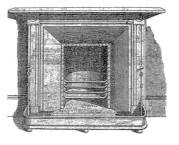

the Rumford grate was immortalized in a gentle Gillray satire. And at about the same time an even more impressive endorsement was penned for this remarkable invention – which, although it was the product of an American brain, was instantly assumed to be a peculiarly British innovation. The General's drawing room described in Jane Austen's *Northanger Abbey* (published in 1817 but written *c.*1798) astonished the heroine Catherine Morland by its modernity – represented by the provision of a Rumford grate only two years after it had first been advocated in print: 'The fire-place, where she had expected the ample width and ponderous carving of former times, was contracted to a Rumford, with slabs of plain though handsome marble, and ornaments over it of the prettiest English china.' In contrast, the mother's secret room, which had barely been touched for years, retained an old-style Bath grate. In this way conservatism and progress were neatly allegorized by the use of fire grates.

Fifteen years after the publication of *Northanger Abbey* British homes were beginning to fit an invention popularized by another famous, polymath American. Back in the mid-eighteenth century, while the British were only just becoming familiar with the hob grate, in the colonies Benjamin Franklin was pioneering the first true warm-air central heating system to be developed since the time of the Roman Empire. Grates were fitted with an empty chamber at the back and air, warmed in this area, was then fed through flues directly into the room. By 1830 'Pennsylvanian fireplaces', as they were invariably called on the other side of the Atlantic, were starting to appear – somewhat belatedly – in British homes, having been common for many years in the United States.

As Catherine Morland's observation reveals, Regency grates were not intended to be purely utilitarian machines but were regarded as stylish pieces of room furniture, too. Many of them were provided with applied ornament in brass or steel – at Temple Newsam in Leeds the 1808 inventory records 'a high-polished steel fender' at the front of a modern grate – and as casting techniques improved, more, finely cast mouldings were added. Attention was thus diverted from the increasingly plain chimney surround to the complex, decorated grate inside it.

At the same time fireplace furniture proliferated. Fire guards, hooked to the top bar of the grate, were widely used and were often decorated with inlaid metal or alloy. Indeed, by 1840 most of the types and designs of fireplace furniture we are now familiar with had come into being: coal-boxes, shovels, tongs, pokers, fire-irons, hearth-brooms, decorated bellows, hearth-stands. Two items common by the 1830s have, though, since disappeared. Fire-screens of green-painted silk, rushes, or canvas – either self-supporting or, more usually, tied to chair-backs – were prevalent, as were bell-pulls – not in themselves connected with the operation of the fire, but invariably placed by the chimney so as to be at the central focus of the room.

Bell-pulls, Southey observed, were generally 'of coloured worsted, about the thickness of a man's wrist' from which were suspended 'knobs of polished

The late eighteenth-century trompe l'oeil *chimneyboard in the Green Damask Room at Temple Newsam, Leeds.*

Opposite: Regency firescreens: three tripod examples and two 'House Fier Screens' – all designs published by Sheraton in 1792 – and (top right) a real-life, japanned example.

spar'. The autocratic German traveller and diarist Prince Pückler-Muskau admired the mechanism which connected the cords to the servants' area, where there were bells 'suspended in a row on the wall, numbered so that it is immediately seen in what room any-one has rung: a sort of pendulum is attached to each which continues to vibrate for ten minutes after the sound has ceased, to remind the sluggish of their duty.'

During the summer, of course, the fireplace could – even in Britain – be dispensed with. The question was then what to put in the gaping hole left by the absence of a cheering fire. Formerly freestanding grates were simply bodily removed, and replaced with a vase of flowers or some such decorative device. With the new, fixed grates, however, a flower-vase, or perhaps a decorated folded fan, was lifted inside the grate bars. An alternative solution was to fix a board over the opening; as was so typical of light-hearted Regency practice, this was often painted with a *trompe-l'œil* representation of the grate behind – even, on occasion, with illusory flowers.

As heat was essential to the British home, so was a supply of water. But unlike the rapid development of the fireplace, the technology of water supply was still in its infancy. Running water on every floor of the house was still a rarity. Indeed, many people still brought their water in jugs from a nearby public pump – a practice which, in time of cholera, ensured that the whole neighbourhood was soon infected with the deadly source of disease. As architectural historian Neil Burton has pointed out, even in a prosperous city such as Bristol only 500 of the 7,000 homes had a piped water supply by 1846.

At the beginning of the period those who did have mains water had it supplied in wooden pipes. New steam pumps, which increased the levels of water pressure, swiftly revealed the inadequacies of the pipe jointing, and serious ruptures were common. An important step forward was made in 1817, however, when the Metropolitan Paving Act stipulated that all water companies were in future to lay cast iron, not wooden, pipes. Even so, many Regency householders could not afford to pay the companies for a 'high service' – the pumping of water to the upper floors. Instead, they settled for the cheaper option of a ground-floor mains supply only and carried water upstairs by hand. The effect of this 'low service' was to inconvenience the inhabitants of the upper floors; in an age where many homes were in multiple occupancy, this further dramatized the social stratifications of the house. As Grose observed in 1795, the 'dignity' of each class of resident in the house was 'in the inverse ratio of altitude'. Servants and upstairs lodgers, faced with the arduous descent for water, were constantly reminded of their lowly social status.

An immediate result of the 1817 act was a sudden increase in the provision of (separate) WCs and bathrooms, at least on the ground floors. In 1778 Joseph Bramah had patented his valve closet WC; this was in fact a variant of Alexander Cummings's 1775 design, but in the event Bramah proved a far better marketing man and by 1797 had sold 6,000 units. This is not to say that WC's were prevalent in Regency Britain. Open drains and

A rare surviving Regency bathroom: the avant-garde 'bamboo bathroom' at Plas Teg in Wales. The early nineteenth-century bath and its integral shower had its own coal-fired hot water supply. The mock-bamboo furniture and the typically Regency yellow walls also date from the first years of the nineteenth century.

cobbled streets still served as handy toilets for much of the population. In 1808 writer James Malcolm lamented that the clientele of inns 'render our streets extremely unpleasant in summer', fastidiously remarking that 'delicacy forbids my adding more on the subject'. Gillray's famous cartoon of the period only begins to suggest the hazards of negotiating what were often virtual open sewers.

Baths and bathrooms were certainly more prevalent than WCs. Most baths were portable, and made of painted wood, sometimes dignified with a marbled finish. The enamelled cast-iron bath, whose descendants now populate so many modern bathrooms, is very much a later, Victorian innovation. Sophisticated washstands, however, were widespread by 1840; indeed, as early as 1790 models were being produced by all the leading ceramic factories. As the years progressed, so they became more intricate, with moulded areas for the water-jug and the soap, as well as a moulded basin, and beneath these fitted compartments for toiletries and shaving equipment. Southey noted in 1807 that 'A compact kind of chest holds the basin, the soap, the tooth brush, and water glass, each in a separate compartment', with mirror, water-jug and bottle, 'and the whole shuts down a-top, and closes in front, like a cabinet.' By 1840 some washstands were being made to fit neatly into bathroom corners; alternatively, large, rectangular models were provided with basic mouldings and designed as the dominant feature of the bathroom.

Unsurprisingly, most Regency bathroom fittings were swept away by the tide of technological advance. With the revival of interest in genuine historic interiors, however, many house owners are attempting to install bathroom fittings with an authentic 'Regency' feel. This is clearly a difficult, indeed almost impossible task. As with lighting, the adoption of historically and socially accurate solutions – be they portable wooden baths, Argand lamps, or gaslights – is simply not practicable, since these types of fittings are either wholly unavailable or, if they can be traced, are prohibitively expensive. Most bathroom or light fittings which claim a pertinent historical pedigree are in fact pseudo-Victorian designs of dubious parentage simply masquerading as 'Regency'.

The relatively simple technological requirements of the Regency bathroom, kitchen, or drawing room are obviously not compatible with today's demands – to say nothing of health, fire, and safety standards. Any pose of 'authenticity' in the context of servicing is bound to involve a large element of compromise; those who energetically espouse a true 'Regency life-style' can all too easily be accused of blatant tokenism. Thus standards other than pure historical precedent must be applied to kitchens and bathrooms in Regency homes. When, for example, choosing bathroom fittings or light switches for a Regency interior, the most important factors to bear in mind are simplicity and sympathy. Bright, over-shined brass designs of an alleged 'Victorian' origin are liable to clash with the quiet restraint of a Regency interior. If in doubt, understated modern examples are often a better choice

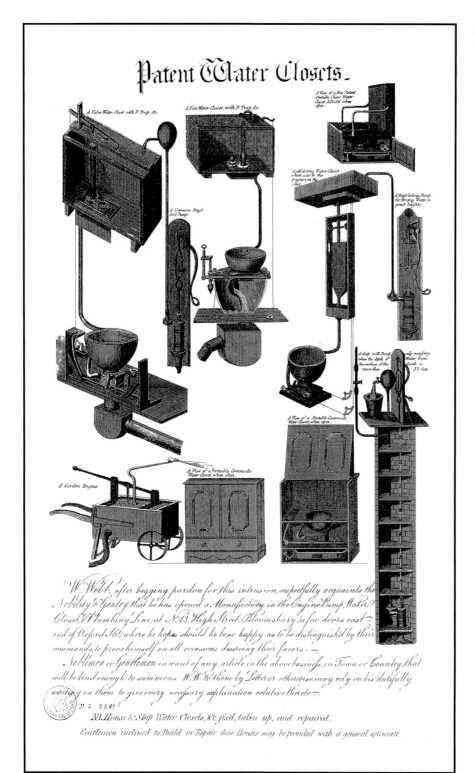

Advanced Regency W.C.s from a contemporary trade card.

A gothic privy from John Plaw's Ferme ornée *of 1795.*

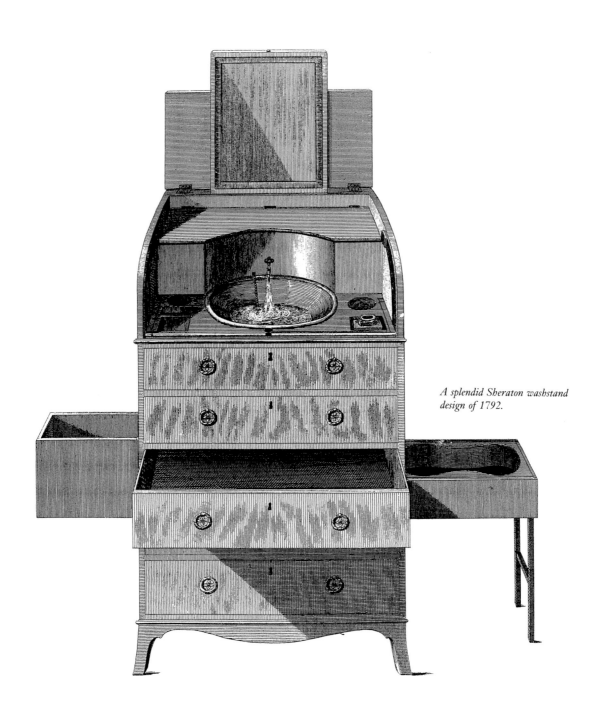

A splendid Sheraton washstand design of 1792.

'The warm bath'. A fascinating and rather melodramatic Regency print with both hot and cold taps in evidence – a rare occurrence for any English home before 1850.

than the pretentious and over-elaborate models labelled as 'traditional'.

One fitting, however, that has not disappeared from the modern home – and is indeed now enjoying a revival in popularity – is the kitchen range. Hot water for the early Regency house was generally brought up from the kitchen, where it was heated in a rectangular boiler, often extended round the back of the fire for more economic heating, and filled and emptied through a lid on the top. John Farey noted that by 1790 'Square iron boilers with lids' had 'spread so amazingly that there is scarcely a house without these'. Soon these boilers were being combined with the grate and the oven in a cast-iron, wood- or coal-fired kitchen range. Ranges first appeared as early as the 1780s: Joseph Langmead's patent range of 1783 effectively provided the basic pattern for ranges for the next two centuries.

Like the fireplace, the range was revolutionized by the energetic genius of Count Rumford. In 1796 the Count observed that 'More fuel is frequently consumed in a kitchen range to boil a tea kettle than with proper management would be sufficient to cook a dinner for fifty men'. Rumford's solution was an almost closed range, with a hotplate for every cooking vessel, which would prevent the heat from soaring up the kitchen chimney.

Rumford's initiative was soon taken up and refined by subsequent inventors. In 1802 George Bodley reduced the grate size still further and covered it with a cast-iron plate, thus launching the first fully closed range. The direct descendant of this – Dr Gustav Dalen's Aga design of 1929 – is still to be seen in many modern British kitchens. In 1833 Loudon reported that locally made closed ranges (marketed as 'Leamington kitcheners') had totally replaced the old-style open ranges in south Warwickshire. Many of

The kitchen at Pickford's House, Friar Gate, Derby, built after 1812. To the left is 'Harrison's Patent Range' of 1820.

Designs from Loudon's Encyclopaedia *of 1833 showing a kitchen range combining boiler and oven ('first made by Mr Eckstein of London') and other simple but technologically advanced kitchen grates.*

these adopted the American fashion of facing the cast-iron frame with grey, brown, or even green soapstone; others risked incorporating native marbles in the design, often inlaid with brass or overlaid with 'English ormolu'. In 1815 Thomas Deakin even produced a 'portable' closed range on iron legs, which could theoretically be brought to the centre of the room. However, unlike the Americans, who took to this invention enthusiastically, the British preferred to loll by the traditional chimney, and these 'American stoves' never gained widespread acceptance in Britain. 'Portable Iron cottage Ovens', declared Loudon in 1833, 'are common among the ironmongers, but they are not very desirable.'

In many humble houses and cottages, of course, cooking was still done over an open hearth (although Loudon hoped that 'the day is not very far distant when open fireplaces will be considered as relics of barbarism'). And not all kitchens were showcases of technology; in 1819 Charles Sylvester moaned that 'Nothing can be more preposterous and inappropriate than the prevailing construction and management of a gentleman's kitchen'. In the more sophisticated homes, however, by 1830 the kitchen was a jumble of impressive machines and mechanisms. Clockwork 'bottle jacks' to turn roasting meat had automatically begun to replace the traditional 'smoke jacks' harnessed to the chimney draught. Cranes for cast iron and, after *c.*1800, copper pots and kettles jostled with pot hooks and chains, as well as with bizarre relics of a more primitive age, such as the 'fire-cat', a pot support, so called because it always landed on its feet. And nowhere was kitchen technology more advanced than at George IV's own Brighton Pavilion, with its highly sophisticated jacks, its impressive rows of copper pots and moulds, and its fabulous decoration. Princess Lieven could not help but be impressed by its 'admirable . . . contrivances for roasting, boiling, baking, stewing, frying, steaming and heating; hot plates, hot closets, hot air, and hot hearths; and all manner of cocks for hot water and cold water'. All this to provide the corpulent King with his fashionably late 6.30 p.m. dinner.

Vying with the range for prominence was that other stalwart of the Regency kitchen, the wooden dresser. Unlike the range, this was not a new invention, but it certainly became more widely used by all social classes during the Regency period. Roughly hewn pine or oak dressers (once again, *always* painted, if not of a demonstrably expensive wood) were ubiquitous by 1830, providing a highly utilitarian base for plate racks, cup hooks, shelves (on which, perhaps, to display one's much-treasured best china), and ample drawer and cupboard space, as well as providing a large work surface. The purposes to which the dresser could be put were legion. Loudon commented in his *Encyclopaedia* of 1833 that dressers were 'essential to every kitchen but more especially to that of the cottage to which they serve both as dressers and sideboards'. And, of course, in sharp contrast to many of the fixtures and fittings of the Regency house, the wooden dresser remains a feature that is still widely available and wholly compatible with the modern household.

Nash's sumptuous Great Kitchen at the Brighton Pavilion. George IV enticed the renowned Carême and other famous French chefs of the day to work here.

'WELL, MR SAWYER', SAID MRS RADDLE, PLANTING HERSELF FIRMLY ON A PURPLE CAULIFLOWER IN THE KIDDERMINSTER CARPET, 'AND WHAT'S THAT TO ME, SIR?'

In 1807 Thomas Hope introduced the term 'Interior Decoration' to the English language and set the tone for an era when, for the first time, interior redecoration and refurbishment became a popular occupation not merely for the grandee but for the average house owner. For the first time there was an array of professional guides available to help the prospective amateur decorator – not only the furniture-oriented pattern-books of Sheraton, Hope, and Smith, but also general guides covering every aspect of the interior. These were usually in the form of a single work or a pair of volumes; Rudolph Ackermann's *Repository of the Arts*, however, inaugurated the fashion for home decoration periodicals which is still thriving today.

These new publications quickly seized on the concept of the planned and co-ordinated interior, and proceeded to exploit it as far as printing technology and the pockets of their readership would allow. In particular, they initiated the concept of the instantly recognizable, comprehensive 'look' to be imposed on all items in the interior. The theory of *en suite* decoration was first pioneered by Ackermann after 1809; by 1833 Loudon was declaring firmly that the colours of an interior should be in 'unison or a proper combination of parts' and that the most common fault in interior decoration was that there was 'no particular tone fixed for an apartment' – an omission which would inevitably result in 'an incongruous mixture'. Carpet colours, asserted Loudon, should always harmonize with the walls and furniture; paintwork was to match the ground of the wallpaper; and the shades and materials of the upholstery should always echo those of the curtains.

To modern ears this may sound obvious; but in the early nineteenth century this doctrine appeared quite revolutionary. Most often it was the colour of the furniture fabrics which dictated the scheme for the whole room. As early as 1789 Gillows were producing a hall floorcloth for a Cumbrian house in which 'the Colours [were] made to suit yr. Furniture'. *En suite* decoration was applicable to every type of room, from those of the grandest mansion to the humble interiors of Mary Ellen Best's York home. This new concept, however, did bring with it certain disadvantages. As Maria Edgeworth noted of her London home in 1818, having – in accordance with

(CHARLES DICKENS, *Pickwick Papers*, 1836–7)

The dark green woodwork in the Morning Room at Pickford's House – a late Georgian town house in the centre of Derby – matches the original colour scheme of c.1825.

Opposite: Repton's graphic demonstration of how a dull and old-fashioned parlour could be dramatically improved by remodelling it in the latest Regency manner. Note the highly fashionable 'clouded' plaster ceiling, the brightly coloured carpet and the prominent link with the richly planted conservatory.

Above: Another Mary Ellen Best view – this time of an interior at Howsham Hall, Yorkshire, of c.1830. There is a marked prevalance of red: on the walls, in the carpet design, and even on the striped furniture covers.

the accepted fashion – covered the footstools with a fabric of the same colours and pattern as the carpet, 'the only inconvenience' was that 'none but lynx eyes can see them and they break all shins'.

The theory of *en suite* decoration did not, however, mean that the whole house was coloured in a uniform manner. The primary function of each room entailed a unique set of decorative prerequisites, to be complemented by appropriately emotive colours. D. R. Hay's *Laws of Harmonious Colouring* of 1829 specified differing, colour-related moods for each room of the house. The drawing room was a place of 'vivacity, gaiety, and light cheerfulness' and should be decorated as such. The dining room should be 'warm, rich, and substantial, with no vivid contrasts'; the library 'solemn and grave'; the bedrooms 'light, clearing, and cheerful'; while 'rather a cool tone' was prescribed for staircases and hallways.

Each of these ambiences corresponded to a different set of colourings taken from a Regency palette which was more vivid, daring, and comprehensive than at any other time during the Georgian era. The colours chosen were not simply derived on pure decorative whim, but had a firm grounding in antique practice; in 1819, for example, C. R. Cockerell's publication of the discoveries at Aegina in Greece, revealing that the walls of ancient Greek buildings had actually not been left as unadorned stone but had been highly coloured, gave the wide range of contemporary colours academic sanction.

In spite of the increasingly large number of colours available, however, one colour was predominant in the principal interiors of Regency Britain: red. Red was held to be the best medium in which to encapsulate the desired effects of richness and liveliness which Hay and others had celebrated. Hay had indeed concluded that 'a proper tint of crimson is the richest and most splendid colour for the walls of a room', being, he added, 'much used in internal decorations'. Red was almost universally recommended for dining rooms, where, in grander houses, the chair upholstery was invariably red leather. Red was also widely believed to be 'the best ground for pictures'; Turner himself strongly advocated red walls as the most suitable background for his paintings, while Sir Thomas Lawrence bemoaned the detrimental effect the new fashion for replacing red with yellow was having on his canvases and gilded picture frames. In 1827 George IV's ageing and unpopular former mistress, the Marchioness of Hertford, took the plunge and replaced the predominantly green interiors at her house, Temple Newsam near Leeds, with red, hanging a rich red damask flock paper in the picture gallery. The reds she used were typical of the time: crimson or ruby, or possibly maroon. Advances in the production of dyes after the Napoleonic Wars, however, produced new variants of red, such as the attractive orange-reds beloved of the more adventurous fabric designers.

While red remained extremely popular in Regency interiors, green was by no means displaced. Greens were much used for drawing rooms and bedrooms and were held to be particularly appropriate for libraries. For his

An intriguing early colour chart from George Smith's Cabinet Maker and Upholsterer's Guide *of 1826–7.*

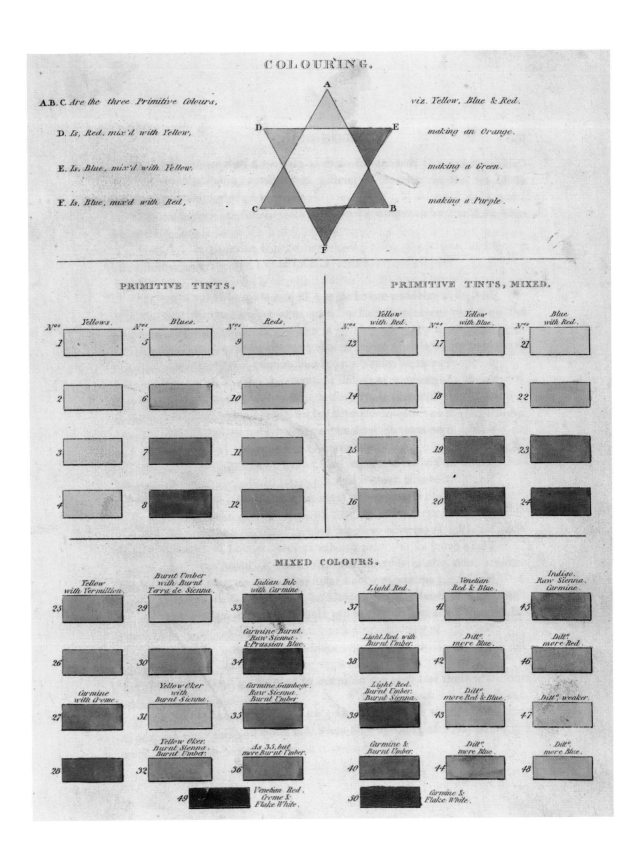

COLOURING.

A.B.C. *Are the three Primitive Colours,*   *viz. Yellow, Blue & Red.*

D. *Is, Red, mix'd with Yellow,*   *making an Orange.*

E. *Is, Blue, mix'd with Yellow,*   *making a Green.*

F. *Is, Blue, mix'd with Red,*   *making a Purple.*

PRIMITIVE TINTS.   PRIMITIVE TINTS, MIXED.

MIXED COLOURS.

Above: Bright red damask is fringed with a strong yellow in this modern recreation of the bed curtains draping Thomas Jefferson's bed at Monticello.

Left: Detail of the 'bronze' green and red colours used by Soane to decorate the Library and Dining Room at 13 Lincoln's Inn Fields. The red was originally more earthy in tone, being derived directly from the 'Pompeian' terracotta-reds being discovered at ancient archaeological sites. Such reds became very popular throughout Europe and America during the first decades of the nineteenth century.

Opposite: The starfish ceiling in the Library at Pitshanger Manor, west London, looks down on the buffs and browns so popular with Soane and his contemporaries. The trellis design was directly copied from the 1790s ceiling at Soane's own London home of 12 Lincoln's Inn Fields.

A heavily-gilded chandelier and ceiling from Lancaster House, London.

Left: The glazed chintz curtains in the South Drawing Room at Sir John Soane's Museum. The bright yellow is designed to match the vivid yellow paint on the walls.

model 'Lake District cottage' of 1818, the architect and designer J. B. Papworth recommended a dark green, trellis-patterned paper in the hallway; a green and buff-painted staircase; a parlour and music room in shades of yellow-green, relieved by a rather alarming pinkish-orange; and a 'tea-green' library. ('Tea-colour' generally referred to the colour of tea leaves, not to the actual drink.) And while many house owners were soon replacing the green paint, paper, or fabrics of their principal rooms with reds, in the manner of Lady Hertford, it must be remembered that the colour green was a constant presence inside and outside the Regency home, being the accustomed colour for all types of utilitarian objects – front doors, woodwork, ironwork, blinds, screens, and so on. Papworth held that 'bronze green' was especially suitable for verandahs and related ironwork since it 'assumes a substantial, though light appearance' and since 'every other colour bespeaks it of wooden construction, and is offensive to the eye of taste.' And in his *Mechanical Exercises* of 1812 Peter Nicholson included more greens than any other colours in his 'List of useful Colours for House Painting', citing 'grass green', verdigris, 'dark ochre green', 'blue-pea', and 'mineral green'. Green was also, as we shall see, the colour of garden rails, fences and gates, and of garden furniture.

While reds and greens were universally used about the house, and blues were usually recommended for bedrooms, the use of yellow was far more controversial. The striking 'Patent Yellow' that Sir John Soane used for the painted walls, curtains, and upholstery of the drawing room at his home in London was as daring then as it appears – excellently restored – today. The Prince of Wales was, typically, very much in the vanguard of fashion when he had Henry Holland fit Carlton House with yellow paper in the library and yellow and maroon paper in the dining room. Yellow remained a controversial colour well into the 1830s; no less a person than the Duke of Wellington was sharply criticized for choosing a yellow paper for the principal rooms of his London home, Apsley House. However, 'drab' colours – which during this period indicated combinations of greeny-yellows, yellow-browns, and yellow-golds – were popular after 1799, in which year Dr Edward Bancroft introduced a new, cheap dye, 'quercitron yellow', made from the bark of the North American oak. Wallpapers printed in these 'drab' colours were particularly common by 1810.

Gold was permitted when part of a drab pattern; in all but the most affluent households, however, gilding was generally avoided, except to enliven furniture woodwork and picture frames. By 1820 the gilt excesses of the Prince Regent at Brighton Pavilion and his brother at Lancaster House were regarded as typical examples of the profligacy of the royal family and of the needless waste of public money, and a puritanical reaction set in. In 1818 Papworth proudly boasted of one of his model homes that 'in the whole of this cottage there is no portion of gilding' and that 'even the book-bindings are unornamented by gold'. As far as the Scot, J. C. Loudon, was concerned, 'gilding, unless in very small quantities for the sake of relief, should be

avoided', for 'if overdone, that which would otherwise have been elegant will become gaudy and vulgar'.

By the time Loudon was writing this in 1833, a distinct trend towards light colours, as well as light materials, was firmly in evidence in interior decoration. Light blues, buffs, lilacs, French greys, and pinks were especially popular, often used in combination with stronger hues of complementary colours. As Hay noted: 'The strength or intensity of a colour is . . . much increased by being placed near its contrasting or accidental tint.' Some of these harmonies were very pleasing; Ackermann particularly recommended the combinations of lilac or fawn with bright green. Others were more unusual, such as T. H. Vanherman's suggestion of 'light yellowish buff' to complement 'light plum colour' for panelling, and Whittock's instructions to obtain a 'flame-colour' effect on the walls by 'drawing a long streak of blue, then one of red, next yellow, and lastly green' on a light ground, after which 'the whole of the streaks are softened and blended together with a large dusting brush'.

The one colour which rarely appeared alone on Regency walls – in sharp contrast to its excessive use today – was white. Early in the nineteenth century chlorine was being newly employed to create bright white, bleached areas in fabric patterns; these were, however, only intended for relief. As Hay wrote in 1829, white was 'seldom employed in house-painting', having 'entirely given way to shades of various colours and imitations of the finer kinds of wood'. Whites were still used for ceilings but even then generally tinted with pinks or blues. (In 1829 Vanherman noted that the brief craze for 'cloud ceilings' in blue and white had 'of late fallen off'.) In the opinion of the furniture-maker George Smith, the use of white by 1828 was simply 'bad taste'.

As already seen, the paint finishes of marbling and graining were all the rage during the Regency period. In 1827 Nathaniel Whittock wrote that: 'The very great improvement that has been made within the last ten years in the art of imitating the grain and colour of various fancy woods and marbles, and the facility and consequent cheapness of this formerly expensive work, has brought it into general use.' He did, however, object to the new idea of marbling furniture: 'nothing can be in worse taste', he fumed, since 'who would choose a marble chair?'

Graining was especially common. In 1829 Vanherman suggested that the technique was going out of fashion, but eleven years later Loudon reported that it was as popular as ever, merely remarking that 'the rage for painting the mouldings in a different kind of wood from the general graining' which had been 'very general some years since' was 'now discontinued'. Graining in imitation of seasoned oak was thought highly appropriate for library woodwork and for the floorboards exposed between the carpet and the skirting. New manuals, such as Whittock's *Decorative Painter's and Glazier's Guide* of 1827, included whole chapters devoted to the different types and techniques of wood graining. The idea even spread beyond the realm of paint finishes: in his *Encyclopaedia* of 1833 Loudon noted the fashion for library

Opposite: 'Grecian' and 'Roman' gilding designs, from Nathaniel Whittock's invaluable Decorative Painter's and Glazier's Guide *of 1827.*

'Satinwood' (above) and 'rosewood' (below) graining examples from Whittock's manual.

*One corner of the Breakfast
Room at Soane's Pitshanger
Manor, west London, built for
his wastrel sons in 1800–03.
This room was restored during
the 1980s by Dr Ian Bristow,
and features the brown 'wood'
tones and marbling so favoured
by early nineteenth-century
designers. The caryatid is
actually not of stone or plaster
but of painted Coade Stone.*

*Typical marbling and graining
designs, as suggested by
Whittock in 1827.*

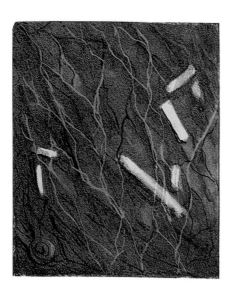
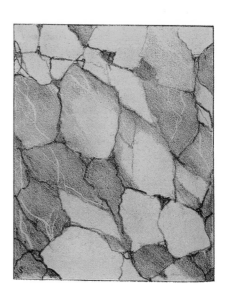

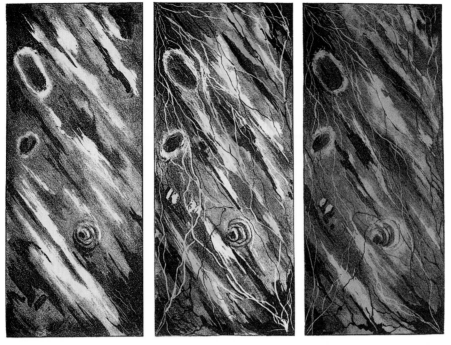

'Verde Antique' marbling, as reproduced by Whittock.

Opposite: American late eighteenth-century stencilled wall decoration, originally from Connecticut but now in the American Museum at Claverton Manor, Bath.

carpets which imitated the 'colour of wainscot' and for oak-grained floorcloths.

Other paint techniques were also used. Stencilling enjoyed a considerable revival in the early nineteenth century: in 1827 Whittock wrote that it was 'the cheapest and most expeditious method of decorating rooms' (adding that it was 'always done with distemper [i.e. size-bound] colours'), while six years later Loudon reported that the practice was 'most common in Britain' and explained how it was done: 'the patterns are all cut out in pasteboard or oilcloth, and as many pieces of board or cloth are employed for each figure, or compartment, as there are colours or shades to be laid on.' Loudon warned, however, that 'in stencilling . . . no figure, however appropriate and beautiful in itself, should be put down at random'. He also noted that, unlike today, the stencilled patterns were always varnished after application.

Paint was, of course, by no means the only finish considered suitable for walls. The use of wallpaper – a very cheap alternative to expensive wall-hung fabrics – was very common in all types of house by 1790. In 1837 Charles Dickens removed the dado rail from the principal rooms of his London home – 48 Doughty Street, in Bloomsbury – so that the new wallpaper could run down to the skirting, a common practice of that time. Four years earlier Loudon noted that 'papering the walls of Rooms is a very general practice in Britain; and is applicable to a certain extent, even to the humblest cottages'; he also observed that 'the variety of papers for rooms is almost endless'.

Wallpaper was still block-printed by hand using carved pearwood blocks and produced in 'pieces' or rolls $11\frac{1}{2}$ yards ($10\frac{1}{2}$ metres) long. It was not until the 1830s that mechanized cylinders were generally substituted for blocks,

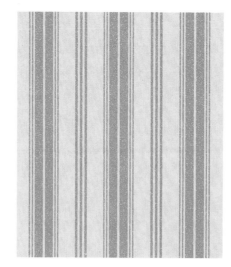

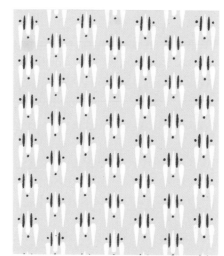

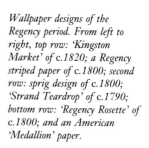

Wallpaper designs of the Regency period. From left to right, top row: 'Kingston Market' of c.1820; a Regency striped paper of c.1800; second row: sprig design of c.1800; 'Strand Teardrop' of c.1790; bottom row: 'Regency Rosette' of c.1800; and an American 'Medallion' paper.

Opposite: Typical wallpaper borders of the Regency period; to their right, an oakleaf design, printed for Clarence House, London, in c.1800.

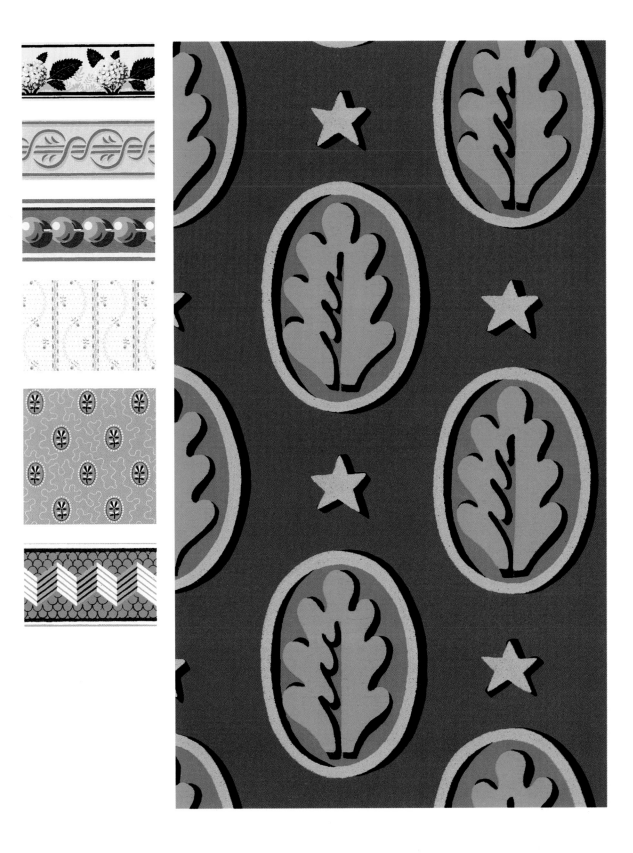

Floral designs were commonly found on Regency wallpapers. Here are a few typical examples. From left to right, top row: 'Oak Garland' of c.1790; 'Bloomsbury Square' of c.1810; second row: 'Fuchsia St James' of c.1835; 'Covent Garden Floral' of c.1830; bottom row: another 'Covent Garden Floral' of c.1830; and 'Pomegranate', a design of the later eighteenth century.

A rare customer pattern book of the 1830s. Made for the Crace family firm, this shows a selection of A. W. N. Pugin's wallpaper and fabric designs for the new Palace of Westminster.

and the first modern-style power-driven rollers did not appear until 1839. In 1783, however, a machine was patented which could emboss paper, and once the ban on imported paper had been lifted in 1825 (and French paper began to flood onto the market) lighter, cheaper paper began to be widely used, poor quality, inferior papers becoming even more prevalent once the longstanding wallpaper tax was abolished in 1836.

Hanging papers was often a job for the specialist. As Sheraton noted in 1803: 'Paper Hangings are a considerable article in the upholstery branch, and being occasionally used for rooms of much elegance, it requires taste and skill rightly to conduct this branch of the business.' By the 1820s wallpaper retailing had become so sophisticated that manufacturers were producing their own, copiously illustrated order books. Cowtan's wonderfully colourful Order Book, which survives in the Victoria and Albert Museum in London, is a particularly marvellous example. The paper samples included in these guides generally reflected current fashion; it is also possible to detect,

*The Chinese Room at Temple
Newsam, Leeds. Redecorated by
Lady Hertford (one of George
IV's ex-mistresses) in 1827–8,
using genuine Chinese
wallpaper – with unsubtly cut-
out additions.*

however, the beginnings of the adoption of a distinct, in-house 'look' by
certain firms, of the kind with which we are very familiar today.

Traditional wallpaper designs were still available. One of the most prized
was flock-paper – paper with powdered wool or other fabric refuse applied
onto glued patterns to give the effect of a cut-pile fabric. Flock-papers were
used for the walls of principal rooms and also for borders. They were not
always appropriate, however: in 1795 Lady Skipwith visited Virginia and
judged that 'velvet paper I think looks too warm for this country', although it
had actually been in widespread use in the United States for over one
hundred years.

Papers imitating marble or dressed stonework were also widely used,
especially for halls and passageways. In 1833 Loudon was writing that 'one of
the best plain papers for the entrance lobby and the staircases of cottages is
one simply marked with lines in imitation of hewn stone'. There were, he
added, also 'very appropriate Gothic papers' available. Papers which
suggested panelling were used in combination with highly decorated paper
borders. Bedrooms were hung with 'moire papers', imitating watered silk, or
with papers suggesting drapery designs. More common in bedrooms,
however, were floral designs or patterns with small repeats – a genre also
very commonly hung in servants' rooms and other more utilitarian areas.
Pin-ground papers were still popular, too – and for very practical reasons: in
1786 an American journal advised readers that 'flies . . . operate to soil paper
in common rooms . . . to prevent which I have pingrounds that fly marks will
not be perceptible upon'. The same retailer also offered 'dark grounds which
the smoke will not considerably affect in the course of twenty years'.

Far more fashionable (and expensive) than pin-ground was imported
Chinese paper – or for those who found this too extravagant but who could
still afford a high-quality paper, an English chinoiserie imitation. In 1806
Prince George presented the mother of his mistress Lady Hertford with a
hand-painted Chinese paper featuring a characteristically Chinese bird-
pattern. In 1827–8 Lady Hertford finally had this hung at Temple Newsam
and, as was often the practice, further embellished it with additional birds
taken from the unused portions of the paper; to the horror of commentators
then and now, however, she also proceeded to stick on engravings of birds
she had cut out from a rare copy of J. J. Audubon's exquisite and now highly
prized *Birds of America*.

Those who could afford real Chinese wallpapers probably owned a
luxury carpet or two. Turkish or Persian carpets were invariably found in the
dining or drawing rooms of the very rich before 1790. However, with the
Regency came not only a sudden increase in carpet ownership, occasioned by
the cheaper methods of industrial production, but also a new preference for
British-made products. This affected rich as well as poor; even George IV
only bought a very few Persian carpets for Brighton Pavilion. By 1840 British
knotted or pile carpets, made by machines that were able to copy the
intricate geometric patterning of the oriental examples, were to be found

Green druggets mark out the path to follow, in order to avoid dirtying the brightly coloured carpet, in this Mary Ellen Best watercolour of the Drawing Room at Naburn, Yorkshire.

Opposite: E. V. Rippingille's The Young Trio *of 1829, all sensibly sitting on a drugget.*

in countless households: no longer were textile floor coverings the preserve of the great country house. Fitted carpets – fitted right up to the edge of the skirting – were very prevalent (in 1812 Peter Nicholson advised that 'doors should be hung so as to rise above the carpet'), although writers such as Loudon favoured a small border of floorboarding of 1'6" – 2' between carpet and skirting. Often the carpet salesman himself fitted them, chalking out the measurements on the floor beforehand. And by the end of the period many of these salesmen were not from upholsterers or furniture-makers but from specialist carpet retailers.

The centre for the manufacture of British knotted carpets, with their bold Neo-Classical patterns, was Axminster in Devon. The factories at Wilton and Kidderminster specialized in woven carpets, with the worsted warp brought to the surface to create a looped pile; this was either left as it was (a so-called 'Brussels' carpet) or cut to produce a velvet-like surface (a 'Wilton' carpet). Brussels and Wiltons were far cheaper and more versatile than Axminsters and other knotted carpets; woven in strips up to three feet wide, they were usually given frequently repeating patterns to enable them to cover all types of areas. They were also generally provided with a wide border and an elaborate fringe.

Echoing the patterns of these carpets was another Regency invention: the hearth-rug, designed to protect the main carpet from wearing out at the busy confluence around the front of the fire. At Attingham Park in 1827 almost every room of consequence possessed fringed hearthrugs; almost at the other end of the social scale, they were depicted in many of Mary Ellen Best's interiors of the late 1830s. In 1807 Southey's *Letters from England* noted not only that 'the whole floor is fitted with carpeting' but that 'before the fire is a

smaller carpet of different fabric, and fleecy appearance . . . a fashion of late
years which has become universal because it is at once ornamental,
comfortable and useful'.

Harder wearing than the pile carpets were the ingrain carpets – so called
because their wool was dyed prior to weaving, and generally known by the
terms 'Kidderminster' or 'Scotch'. They were made by intersecting two webs
of cloth, using the same principle as damask; on the back, the pattern would
be identical to the front, but the colours exactly reversed. In 1822 three-ply
ingrains were first woven at Kilmarnock in Scotland; this innovation allowed
for more complex and colourful designs, with backs and fronts that were
wholly different. Ingrain carpets were popularly regarded as coarse and
cheap; yet they served very well as utilitarian coverings for hallways, servants'
rooms, and stairs. ('Stair carpets give an air of great comfort and finish to a
house', advised Loudon, 'and a cottage should never be without one.')

Even more basic – and more widespread – than ingrain carpets were
druggets and their whole family of related floor and carpet covers. When
ordering a carpet from Haig and Chippendale in 1789, a client specifically
stipulated that 'there must be a covering for it of green serge'. Although
other colours – particularly brown – were used, green was the most
widespread colour used for these simple textile coverings. Often they were
enlivened by needlework borders – which have often survived after the
drugget itself has perished. Made from baize (a heavy woollen cloth), serge
(a twilled worsted fabric), haircloth (spun animal hair combined with a cotton,
linen, or wool warp), or similar heavy-duty materials, they were principally
used to protect fine carpets from dirt and wear, often being attached to floor
studs to prevent them wrinkling. (The decision whether or not to remove the
drugget from the Axminster or Wilton let you know exactly how important a
guest you really were.) Druggets were there to catch crumbs, to catch falling
soot, even to catch hair powder. In poorer households, of course, they were
used as substitutes, not covers, for good carpets; as Loudon commented, they
were 'not only cheap, but in many cases look remarkably well'.

The long-established alternative to drugget was the simple painted
floorcloth or oilcloth. In 1812 the American Hezekiah Reynolds's *Directions
for House and Ship Painting* explained how these were made: 'Canvas or
common tow cloth is sewed with a flat seam, of the dimensions required; and
nailed firm upon a floor; then wet with water even, and thoroughly; and
before dry, is primed with any common colour.' After two more coats of
paint, and the filling of any cracks with putty, the cloth was 'divided into
squares or diamonds of which one half . . . are painted white; and the other
half black'.

In 1816 the painter Rolinda Sharples provided directions for a more
durable pattern, by which the colour was stamped, hot, onto the cloth with a
pearwood block, and 'when it is finished breadth ways with one colour, it is
stamped with another, the pattern of the former, until completed'.
Floorcloths did not just imitate black and white marble flooring. Loudon

*An extremely rare survivor: a
late eighteenth-century
floorcloth – painted to resemble
tessellated marble blocks – found
at Calke Abbey in Derbyshire.*

Detail of one of the cloak pins used to fasten the curtains in the South Drawing Room at Sir John Soane's Museum.

mentions patterns of stones, wainscot, and 'tessellated pavement' (of the kind found at Calke Abbey in Derbyshire), while the Attingham sale catalogue of 1827 included 'a piece Turkey-pattern Floor-Cloth', actually attempting to mimic a luxury carpet. To match his oak-coloured drugget at Abbotsford, Sir Walter Scott bought an oak-coloured oilcloth, which he wisely placed under the sideboard to catch spillages. By 1821 the floorcloth-makers Smith and Barber, according to paint expert Dr Ian Bristow, were offering 'Plain Red', 'Yellow Mat', 'Green Mat', 'Alex. Pavement', 'Octagon Marble', 'Patera', 'Tessellated mble.', 'Fancy Flower', 'Oak Leaf', 'Foliage', 'Carlton', 'Green Cluster', 'Imperial', 'Turkey', and 'Persian' floorcloths. Dr Bristow also notes that floorcloths – 'not economical articles', as Loudon said, 'where there is much going out and coming in of persons generally employed in the open air, and of course wearing strong shoes' – often did not last long, and many tradesmen were soon offering a sideline of 'Old Cloths new Painted and Repair'd'.

In 1833 Loudon also noted a close relation of the floorcloth, the 'paper carpet'. No examples survive, but they were apparently made by sewing together pieces of paper, or rough cloth, which were then varnished, oiled, and painted. The finished product could then be rolled up and stored.

The Regency interest in chinoiserie also helped to promote a dramatic revival in the provision of oriental-style matting on floors. No longer was reed, cane, or rush matting simply a covering to be used on floors in the most modest cottages and farmhouses. The Prince of Wales himself – once again anticipating fashion – even put rush matting into the luxurious and sophisticated environment of the Great Drawing Room at Carlton House.

The element of the Regency interior whose development was most profoundly affected by the Industrial Revolution was the family of furnishing fabrics. The cylinder printing of fabrics was first patented by Thomas Bell in 1783 and was widespread by 1810. Even more importantly, in 1801 a revolutionary new loom was invented by the Frenchman Jean-Marie Jacquard which, by replacing much of the effort of human labour by a series of punched cards, enabled complex patterns to be produced on a large scale and, once the initial investment on the cards and machinery had been recouped, very cheaply. In 1820, in a reinterpretation of the spirit of Waterloo, the Englishman Stephen Wilson employed an industrial spy to find out exactly how Jacquard's invention worked, and – to a collective sigh of relief from the British textile industry – the following year was able to issue a British patent for a similar system. By 1830 Jacquard weaves were beginning to appear in Britain and America; as textile historian Mary Schoeser has noted, these 'muscular' new designs 'were often vigorously shaped or broken by strong outlines' and frequently copied French patterns of the period.

Most significant of all was the huge growth in the fortunes of cotton. With Cartwright's power loom of 1787 and Whitney's cotton gin of 1793, the manufacture of cotton fabrics was quickly able to overtake and eclipse that of other traditional furnishing materials. Cotton chintzes and calicoes of

Drapery detail from Lancaster House. The gold-coloured fabric, designed to match the gilded pelmet, was very fashionable in the early nineteenth century.

Left: Regency Chinoiserie. The interior of the Chinese Room at Middleton Park, Oxfordshire. Refitted during the remodelling of 1806–10 for the Prince of Wales's former mistress, Lady Jersey. The elaborately-draped curtains frame the view through to the conservatory in the best Regency manner; their purple colour shows how daring Regency decorators could be.

A Rudolf Ackermann design for window drapery, with simply-embroidered muslin sub-curtains, of 1815.

all grades were quickly available, and chintzes and other cotton fabrics of greater sophistication soon displaced the more expensive silks as essential fabrics for the interior. The immediate result of this development was that the Spitalfields silk industry was soon in dire straits; in 1816 Ackermann specifically urged the use of silks in bedrooms in order to help revive 'the present state of our silk-manufactories'.

Cotton fabrics particularly helped satisfy the new demand for lighter, washable furnishing materials. Heavy, traditional fabrics such as moreen ('apt to harbour moths and other vermin', noted Loudon in passing) were being discarded in favour of washable chintzes in bedrooms all over Britain. Already in 1807 Southey reported that 'damask curtains which were used in the last generation have given place to linens' which were more easily washable – silks or satin failing to give 'that clean appearance which the English always require'. For households of limited means, white dimity – washable, plain, and simple to border – was invariably chosen for curtains and bed-hangings. And even the more exotic fabrics were now within easy reach of most purses. Merino was a popular new material made from the superb wool of Spanish merino sheep, introduced into Britain by George III himself in 1786; its relative cheapness soon prompted authors such as Ackermann to recommend it as a substitute for dearer silks or superfine cloths. Even cheaper were the new 'Manchester velvets' – cottons with small diaper patterns that were stamped by machine – and the machine-pressed 'watered' fabrics.

Chintz, however, remained the most successful of all the new cottons. Glazed or unglazed, it could be used for bed hangings or window curtains, for loose covers or upholstery. It was cheap, and it was washable. And (so Ackermann noted in 1809) as the novelty of the early, brightly coloured British chintzes faded, so 'the gaudy colours of the chintz and calico furniture' gave way 'to a more chaste style, in which two colours only are employed to produce that appearance of damask'.

Geometrical or architectural patterns were still hugely popular, often as a background for multicoloured figurative designs. Trelliswork, pillars, and stripes were particularly prevalent; and although, ironically, what is now generally known as the 'Regency stripe' pattern was not revived until 1824, half-way into the period, by 1830 striped cotton or linen upholstery or loose covers were in evidence in countless homes.

The bedroom in particular represented a showcase for every variety of furnishing fabric, George Hepplewhite remarking in 1794 that bed hangings alone could be 'of almost every stuff which the loom produces'. Few examples of Regency bed drapery survive today, but from original prints it can be seen that in grander bedrooms some displays were very elaborate indeed, the fabric being draped in luxurious fashion around the tester and posts. (With the continued provision of candles such arrangements were, of course, a serious fire hazard, and bedroom fires were very common throughout the period.) The drapes were generally coloured, and lined with a

Opposite: an ambitious curtain design, published by George Smith in 1826. Note the highly fashionable prominence of the curtain rod.

Designs by Loudon of 1833 for simple window treatments.

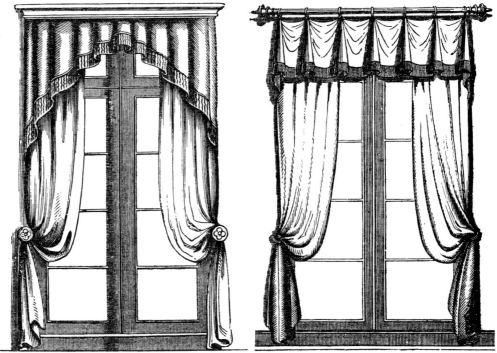

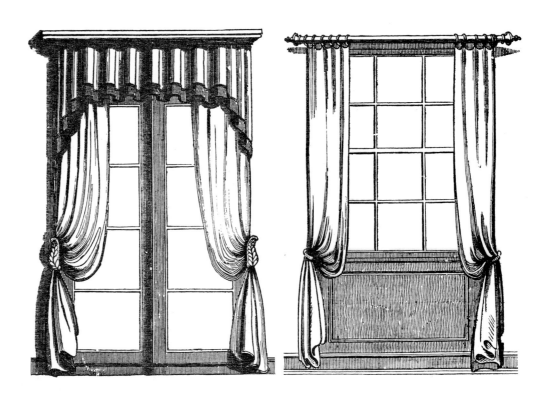

material of different but harmonizing tone, either plain or spotted. To enliven the ensemble further, the rear bed curtain was frequently arranged in a semicircular, sunburst pattern. The materials on the mattress itself, however, were invariably white or undyed. Robert Southey's fictional Spanish tourist remarked in 1807 that blankets 'are of the natural colour of the wool, quite plain; the sheets plain also. I have never seen them flounced nor laced, nor ever seen a striped or coloured blanket'. The counterpane or bedspread, he further observed, was 'of white cotton' and could well have been of the popular quilted cotton variety.

In smaller homes window curtains, too, would often be white; made of dimity and possibly provided with a shawl, or even a paper border, they could, condescended Loudon, be 'put up with a degree of style and taste which indicates both talent and a love of home in the occupant'. Where the householder was rich enough, however, window curtains – of plain or printed cottons, or even of silk – were always interestingly coloured and, as Southey's Don Manuel reported of his 'rich printed cotton' curtains, 'lined with a plain colour and fringed'. Elaborately draped and extending to floor length – even trailing on the ground – to accommodate the newly fashionable floor-length windows, in many houses they represented the decorative focus of the Regency room. A drawing room was frequently judged by the sophistication of its curtains – which, declared Loudon, 'give the mistress of the house an excellent opportunity of exercising her taste in their arrangement'. Those that could be drawn were looped back during the day at dado level and held with pins or cords; many curtains of the period, however, were not designed to be moved, and were simply devised as static displays of colourful drapery. By 1840 these displays had become far less pretentious and expensive, the main aim of the 'mistress of the house' being, as Loudon explained, to display the fabric 'without too much obstructing the light' (a practical consideration all too quickly forgotten by many of today's decorating enthusiasts).

Despite the modern belief to the contrary, by 1800 the vertically drawn festoon curtain (now known by a variety of alternative names, ranging from 'ruched blind' to the rather more irreverent but possibly more appropriate 'tart's knickers') was wholly out of fashion. 'These curtains are still in use in bedrooms', commented Sheraton in 1803, but he marked 'the general introduction of the French rod curtain in most genteel homes'. The modern-style 'French rod' system first appeared in the 1780s: the hangings drew horizontally, not vertically, and were suspended from wood or brass curtain rods with clamps at either end, which were decorated and left exposed (with rosettes or tassels marking where the fabric was tethered) or hidden behind a pelmet or valance. Each of the rings was connected to strings attached to a pulley, the whole drawing mechanism being operated from the dado rail.

These curtains could be hung singly or doubly, in the modern fashion; if in the 'Gothic style', the valance formed a (very approximate) Gothic arch. When drapery displays were at their most elaborate at the beginning

A green-painted Venetian blind, now in the American Museum at Claverton Manor, Bath. Green blinds such as this were very common in British and American homes of the Regency era.

of the nineteenth century, some rooms were fitted with what was called 'continuous drapery', where the window drapes ran in massive swags from pelmet to pelmet (or 'curtain cornice' as it was sometimes known). In extreme cases even the ceiling was draped, too, creating an effect neatly described by the term 'tent-room'.

As the period progressed, not only did Regency householders tire of these overt displays of fabric but the materials and the colours used for the curtains became lighter. Rich, heavy, red curtains remained traditional for the library and dining room. However, as early as 1808 George Smith testified that dull gold 'tabby' silk, with alternate satin and 'watered' stripes, was very commonly used for drawing room curtains. And by 1830 lighter blues, lilacs, and fawns were all very much in vogue. These colours were usually augmented by a decorative border. As textile historian Karin Walton has explained, 'festoon curtains, which spent much of the time bunched up across the top of the window, were not suited to bordering'; thus the disappearance of the festoon naturally encouraged a great vogue for specially printed or sewn borders. By 1792 firms were supplying matching bordered curtains and chair cases; by 1810 even exotic black sewn borders were much in evidence.

Behind the principal curtains – particularly if they could not actually be drawn – was a complex system of sub-curtains and blinds whose main function was not to retain heat (the window shutters did that at night) but to filter daylight and thus protect the cherished furniture, fabrics, and paintings within the rooms from serious damage. Muslin sub-curtains were ubiquitous in the Regency home. They were usually white, but sometimes tinted or provided with an embroidered, geometric-pattern border. They were often used in combination with blinds, which could be of the roller, Venetian, slat, or wire varieties, or simply of stretched fabric or paper. Roller blinds were the height of fashion in the early nineteenth century; originally simply linen or a similar material nailed to a cylindrical piece of wood, by the 1830s the rollers, Loudon explained, comprised 'a tin case that encloses a spring, which acts so as to turn the roller, and pull up the blind itself'. There is some evidence to suggest that some houses were provided with heavy external roller blinds, too; from the very few examples which have survived, these appear to have been of a stout, striped canvas.

Static blinds were more common in poorer households. These consisted of green-painted canvas or wire stretched over a wooden frame, or perhaps the more sophisticated frame-and-lath blinds whose slats, as Thomas Martin explained in 1813, could be made to move 'by turning a brass knob at the upper side of the frame'. In recent years English Heritage's Treve Rosoman rescued three rare examples of this type of blind from a house in Hackney, east London; their frames, he discovered, were mahogany, and the laths (and not silk strips, as originally believed) were painted light green. Green was indeed a common colour for painted blinds, as it was for external shutters (although in 1808 George Smith somewhat sensibly recommended that roller blinds be painted 'of the same colour as the principal draperies'). Not all

blinds were painted one, flat colour, however. The practice of painting blinds
and screens with transparent scenes was one which was actually far more
common in the United States than in Early Regency Britain, but which by
the end of the period had gained widespread acceptance on both sides of the
Atlantic. The idea, as expounded in Edward Orme's *Essay on Transparent
Prints* of 1807, was 'to supply the place of painted glass'. Classical scenes or
rural panoramas were the most popular subjects, although Orme
enthusiastically recommended the depiction of fashionable Chinese figures in
the manner of Brighton Pavilion ('which palace', he fawned, 'his Royal
Highness has fitted up with all the elegance of refined taste').

Blinds and muslin curtains were expressly designed to prevent direct light
from fading precious elements of the interior. In the same vein, much of the
furniture of the period was almost permanently clothed with loose covers.
Glazed chintz, calico, green baize, gingham, and leather covers were very
common, as almost any painting of the rooms of the period will show, and
were *not*, as is often believed, a Victorian innovation. As Karin Walton has
remarked, much of the time Regency interiors remained 'shrouded in serge
and linen'. Needlework covers were out of fashion, although they later
became a characteristically Victorian taste. The anonymous author of the
Workwoman's Guide of 1838 suggested chintz, Holland, or calico covers –
'with or without piping . . . lined with thin glazed calico', and tightly
fastened with sewn loops and strings. Nor were loose covers solely for seating
furniture: in 1803 Sheraton cited 'covers for pier tables, made of stamped
leather and glazed, lined with flannel to save the varnish of such table tops',
adding that 'lately they have introduced a new kind of painted canvas' to
serve the same purpose. Richer families could afford damask protective covers
for their tables and sideboards; tablecloths, the *Workwoman's Guide*
confidently averred, were always of damask.

Under the loose covers the upholstery for chairs and sofas was generally
of the same materials and colours as the curtains. The new cotton chintzes,
with their large and colourful designs and their washability were, again, very
popular, the most important motifs always being placed on the back, where
they were more visible than if on the seat. Leather, though, remained the
accustomed covering for dining room and library chairs. In addition to the
application of borders in strong colours, fringes and tassels proliferated –
often (if it could be afforded) of gold or silver thread. Sofas and settees were
sometimes covered with the most opulent materials – possibly satins or
damasks – and, in addition to their tasselled bolsters and fringes, were often
provided with decorative tufts – buttoning being very much a Victorian
practice. Nor was the display of drapery limited to the windows: in the more
ostentatious homes drapery was suspended from the arms, backs, and rails of
seating furniture and from tables. A wealth of highly decorated and exotically
coloured fabrics awaited the visitor who was brave enough to peek beneath
the loose covers.

*Previous two pages: Examples
of designs for transparent
painted blinds from Whittock's
house decorators' manual of
1827.*

*Opposite: An elaborate classical
scene is the subject of another of
Whittock's painted blinds.*

THERE IS IN ENGLAND, WE BELIEVE, A PRETTY GENERAL CONTEMPT FOR THOSE WHO ARE HABITUALLY AND SERIOUSLY OCCUPIED ABOUT ... PALTRY AND FANTASTICAL LUXURIES; AND AT SUCH A MOMENT AS THE PRESENT, WE CONFESS WE ARE NOT A LITTLE PROUD OF THIS ROMAN SPIRIT, WHICH LEAVES THE STUDY OF THOSE EFFEMINATE ELEGANCIES TO SLAVES AND FOREIGNERS, AND HOLDS IT BENEATH THE DIGNITY OF A FREE MAN TO BE EMINENTLY SKILLED IN THE DECORATION OF COUCHES AND THE MOUNTING OF CHANDELIERS.

(SYDNEY SMITH, 1807)

The stunningly over-gilded Blue Velvet Room from the Prince of Wales's Carlton House, depicted by Pyne in c.1818. Holland's original interior of the 1780s was redecorated by the Prince in 1795, in 1806 and again after 1809, when the 'garter-blue' velvets and the blue-ground fleur-de-lis satins seen here were delivered. Most of the room's furniture was designed by Tatham, who also replaced the white lutestring curtains with gold satin ones.

The most typical and easily recognizable element of any English Regency interior – whether in London or Newcastle or transported to Paris or New York – was its furniture. This was not only due to the manner in which the pieces were designed and manufactured. Two key prerequisites helped to make this aspect of the Regency interior more distinct and more daring than in the furniture of any previous age of English interior design: the new precedence of informality and the sudden proliferation of exotic and unorthodox styles.

The importance of the new, informal arrangement of fashionable interiors both large and small cannot be overstated. For the first time in the history of the English interior, pieces of furniture were not stacked up against the walls in stiff, serried ranks after use, but remained disposed about the whole room in a free and easy – and decidedly asymmetrical – fashion.

Portrait of Charles Dickens by Maclise, of 1839. Note the sinuous lines of his Regency chair.

A page of cornice designs from Thomas Sheraton's The Cabinet Maker and Upholsterer's Drawing Book, *1791–3.*

The consequent liberation of the interior was shockingly dramatic. It greatly appealed to observers such as Jane Austen, who, in her novel *Persuasion* of 1816, approved of the fact that 'the present daughters of the house were giving the proper air of confusion by . . . little tables, placed in every direction'. But it was not an innovation that aesthetic conservatives could stomach. In 1811 the American Louis Simond visited Osterley Park, to the west of London, and was horrified to find that

tables, sofas and chairs were studiously deranged about the fire-places and in the middle of the rooms, as if the family had just left them. Such is the modern fashion of placing furniture carried to an extreme, as fashions are always, that make the apartments of a fashionable house look like an upholsterer's or cabinet-maker's shop.

This new development was particularly apt for smaller households, which lacked sufficient numbers of servants continually to rearrange furniture. It also corresponded well with those other trends to informality in the Regency house – encouraging more light, and more plants, in the interior.

Along with informality went simplicity. Basic, geometric forms were now in vogue – not the over-decorated, delicate fripperies of the Rococo and Adam periods. Regency furniture was simple and substantial, with bold curves, unbroken lines, and restricted ornament. This philosophy was first set out in the 1780s and 1790s by Henry Holland, in his designs for the Prince of Wales's Carlton House and subsequently for Southill Park in Bedfordshire, and by the early nineteenth century it was widely accepted. In 1809 Ackermann noted that 'the heavy and cumbrous objects of furniture are giving place to airy and lighter designs' and sixteen years later was eulogizing French-style furniture for employing an 'open and delicate' form in order to achieve the desired 'effect of lightness'.

At the same time the design of furniture was liberated from many of the eighteenth century's conventions and dictates. As the period progressed, the multiplication of exotic styles became almost bewildering. And no style was so astoundingly different, and none so immediately influential, as the Graeco-Egyptian Neo-Classicism of Thomas Hope. Hope, a Dutch refugee from the incursions of the French army, settled in London in 1795, and only twelve years later produced in *Household Furniture and Interior Decoration*, a pattern-book which, to use his own words, introduced 'a totally new style of decoration'. The Egyptian interiors of Hope's own London home in Duchess Street, which formed such an important part of the work, were hailed by Benjamin West as 'the finest specimen of true taste . . . either in England or in France'. Hope's disciplined line drawings successfully communicated the austerity, bulkiness, and simplicity of his furniture and interiors – while, it must be admitted, failing to give any impression of the vivid blues, oranges, and blacks which he advocated for them.

Unsurprisingly, they also gave offence to many. Sydney Smith's *Edinburgh Review* analysis of July 1807 was an especially savage indictment. 'Mr Hope is a great advocate of solidity', he began with some justification,

This gilded and ebonized Egyptian sofa with winged sphinxes is very much in the brilliant if ponderous manner of Hope and Tatham.

A design by Gillows for a canopied 'Egyptian' bedhead. This type of Egyptian-style furniture was very popular during the first quarter of the nineteenth century. Ironically, though, the origin of the Regency sphynx motif may have actually been Greek not Egyptian; architectural historian Patrick Conner has pointed out that the sphynxes normally portrayed by Regency designers are female Grecian examples.

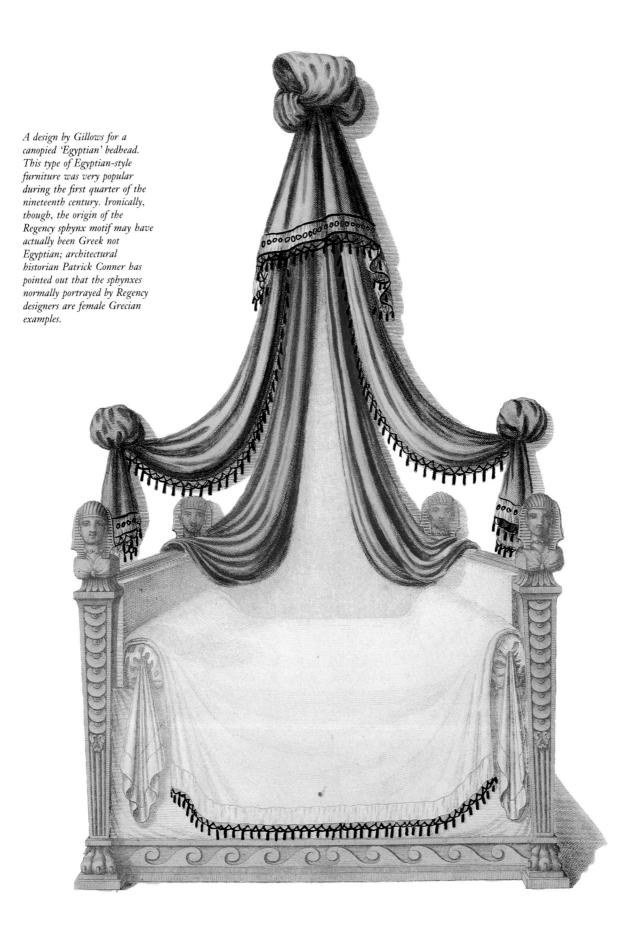

'and has produced such an assemblage of squared timber, and massive brass, as would weigh down the floor and crush out the walls.' Smith then proceeded to castigate every aspect of the book, most notably Hope's use of animal and mythological motifs to decorate his furniture (a decorative theme which had already been prominently employed by Sheraton and Tatham). 'By virtue of what analogy', he thundered, 'is a griffin or a chimera introduced to support a dressing table? – or what has a lion's head to do on the pediment of a sofa, and a man's bust on the cover?' Smith's conclusion was that Hope's furniture was 'affected, pedantic, and unnatural'. The architect Charles Busby also declared in the following year that: 'Of all the vanities which a sickly fashion has produced, the Egyptian style . . . appears the most absurd; a style which, for domestic buildings, borders on the monstrous.'

Hope's innovations survived the onslaught – not, however, through the medium of his own *Household Furniture* (Sydney Smith was correct when he pointed out that the high cost of the book 'puts it out of the reach of the ordinary reader') but through the popularity of George Smith's similarly titled work of 1808. Before Hope, Thomas Sheraton had done much to popularize the new trend to 'Grecian' forms in furniture. His *Cabinet Dictionary* of 1803 was hugely important, not only because it provided British cabinetmakers with practical examples of the new styles, but because it spread this French-influenced but quintessentially English synthesis of austerity and simplicity abroad – Sheraton's sales in Federalist America proving particularly encouraging.

It was George Smith, however, who brought the innovations and novelties of English Regency furniture within the grasp of a mass audience on both sides of the Atlantic. He simplified and rationalized Hope's precise and academic forms to make them more palatable to the average householder and more within the capabilities of the average cabinetmaker. The 'Egyptian' style was diluted to an extent where, as furniture expert Frances Collard has noted, it 'often amounted to no more than the addition of a crocodile, serpent or Sphinx-head to pieces of otherwise conventional Greek Revival form'. Smith also took care to make his work cheaper – while directly borrowing his title from Hope as a cunning piece of elementary marketing. The result was, in the words of a recent American critic, 'the most comprehensive pattern-book of the time'.

The stylistic development of Regency furniture which Hope, Sheraton, Smith, and their fellow designers had provoked was profound. As early as 1809 Ackermann was highlighting 'the revolution which has, within these few years, taken place in the furniture and decorations of the apartments of people of fashion . . . by the study of the antique'. It was not only the ancient worlds of Greece and Egypt, however, which served as models for Regency interiors. By the mid-1820s a Gothic style of somewhat more precision than the fanciful Gothick of the eighteenth century, but still far more light-hearted in tone than the products of the earnest Victorian Goths, was beginning to be used for everyday furniture as well as for grand baronial

Opposite: Some splendid designs from Ackermann's Repository *of 1809: (above) drawing room furniture, and (below) 'Ladies Toilette, Fauteuil, Footstool etc'. These were among the first designs to be published by Ackermann; the* Repository of the Arts *continued to appear for the next nineteen years.*

Right: Two elaborate candelabra and (centre) two tripod stands for vases, as reproduced in George Smith's influential The Cabinet-Maker and Upholsterer's Guide, *published in 1826.*

retreats. George Smith was the first designer to feature a complete range of Gothic furniture; most of the Gothic plates of his *Household Furniture* of 1808 were, however, more reminiscent of the skin-deep Gothick of Strawberry Hill and Inveraray Castle than of truly medieval forms. Two years later Smith himself was actually warning in the *Repository* that only the rich could afford to indulge in Gothic fantasies, since 'no person of a genuine taste' should be seen to introduce isolated examples of Gothic furniture into a house that had not been wholly Gothicized; the result, he claimed, would be 'grotesque and ridiculous'.

But the popular interest in Gothic did not abate – fuelled as it was by contemporary Gothic romances in both literary and architectural forms. In 1825 Ackermann judged the time was right to exploit the passion for Gothic romance, mystery, and historicism and included in his *Repository* a series of designs for Gothic furniture by A. C. Pugin. Accompanying them were claims that 'the architecture of the middle ages possesses more playfulness in its outline, and richness in its details than any other style' – hardly the sentiments of the committed Victorian Gothicist but an invocation calculated to appeal to the more frivolous spirit of the Regency. The designs were so successful that, shortly after the end of the series, they were reprinted in a single volume under Pugin's own name, simply entitled *Gothic Furniture*. The fashion for 'medieval' furniture spread like wildfire – particularly into libraries and halls, undoubtedly on account of the vaguely monkish and ceremonial connotations of these rooms. As early as 1827 Ackermann was noting that 'we have now so many skilful workers in Gothic that very elaborate pieces of furniture may be made at a moderate price'.

In contrast to the architects and theorists of the mid-Victorian era, Regency designers felt no allegiance to any particular period of Gothic design. However, by 1830 there was evolving a distinct preference for the 'Elizabethan' style – an eclectic and decidedly unacademic combination of fifteenth-century, Tudor, and Jacobean forms which was no doubt chosen to recall the glories of the Elizabethan age (and, indeed, to reflect on Britain's current political pre-eminence). Since little sixteenth-century furniture actually survived, there were few models available, and thus, rather as had been the case with the 'Chinese taste', designers were able to let their imaginations run riot.

The results, alas, were often rather uncomfortable – both visually and practically. Loudon warned that, while a Greek chair ought to be 'prized for its expression . . . for its simplicity, and for the great effect produced in it by a very few lines', the Elizabethan chair 'wants that beauty of simplicity, or that evidence of effecting the most important ends by the simplest means'. Elizabethan furniture, Loudon admitted in 1833, was 'sometimes very rudely composed', while the architect C. R. Cockerell – himself no stranger to stylistic experiment – noted in passing that most so-called 'Tudor' furniture was 'undoubtedly of spurious origin'.

Even more abhorrent to the aesthetic purist was the popular resurgence

George Smith's designs of 1826 for a wide variety of Regency table legs.

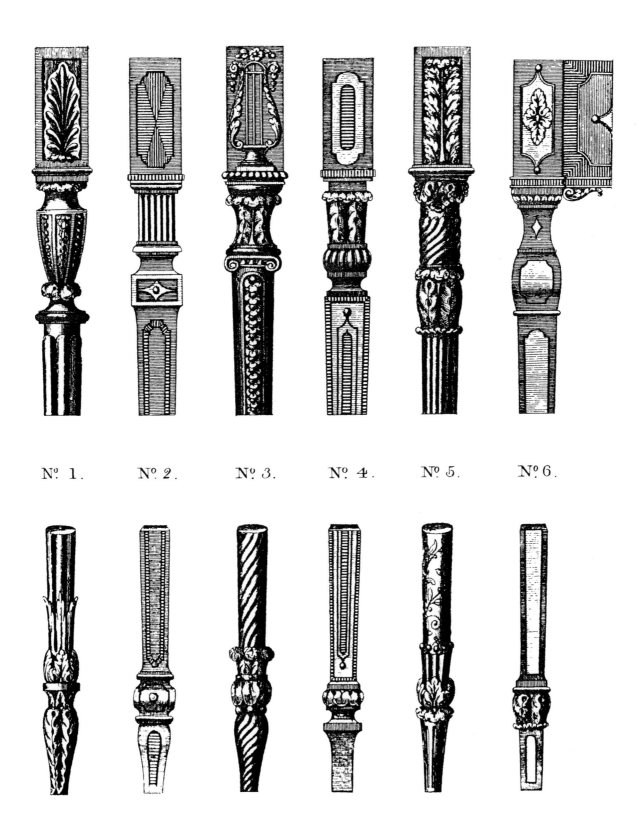

Nọ 1.   Nọ 2.   Nọ 3.   Nọ 4.   Nọ 5.   Nọ 6.

Opposite: Variations on the theme: further elaborate table legs from Smith's Cabinet-Maker and Upholsterer's Guide.

'Pillars for Tables and Stands' from Sheraton's The Cabinet-Maker and Upholsterer's Drawing Book, *published in forty-nine parts between 1791 and 1794. Within a decade of producing this stunningly original work, Sheraton was on the verge of insanity, and died in 1806 without completing his last book,* The Cabinet-Maker; Upholsterer; and General Artist's Encyclopaedia.

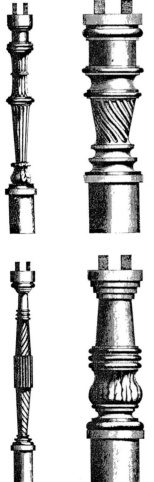

of French fashions which followed the conclusion of peace at Vienna in 1815. In 1822 Ackermann observed that 'the Taste for French furniture is carried to such an extent, that most elegantly furnished mansions . . . are fitted up in French style'. This fad – originally inspired by the passion of the Prince Regent for French furniture – brought in its wake countless over-decorated and badly made pieces, allegedly reviving the styles of Louis XIV or Louis XV, which represented the exact antithesis of Hope and Sheraton's doctrine of pure, clean lines. Hope himself had no sympathy with this style: 'that degraded French school of the middle of the last century', he termed it, which had been 'totally destitute of . . . true elegance and beauty'.

Yet in spite of Hope's pleas, stylistic pluralism became the hallmark of late Regency furniture. By the mid-1820s countless 'historical' styles were vying for attention. In the wake of orthodox Greek, Graeco-Egyptian (now, in fact, decidedly on the wane), Louis XIV, Gothic, and the newer fad for 'Elizabethan', came stranger styles still. Walter Scott's hugely successful novel *Ivanhoe* helped to promote a short-lived Norman Revival – originally and confusingly termed the 'Saxon Style', no doubt in deference to the nationalistic sympathies of Scott's work. There was also, of course, a marked enthusiasm for the 'Chinese' style, a passion which had never really gone away since the mid-eighteenth century but which received an added impetus from the elaborate Chinese furniture George IV had especially made by Crace and Jones for the Brighton Pavilion. And even more obscure nationalities were quoted. Hope himself, in his Duchess Street house, included furniture not only in the 'Chinese' style but in 'Turkish' and 'Hindu', too. The overall effect on those who were not regular readers of the *Repository* could be quite bewildering. 'Only think of a crocodile couch and sphinx sofa!' exclaimed Miss Mitford in 1819, 'They sleep in Turkish tents and dine in a Gothic chapel . . . and all manner of anomalies are the consequence.'

Regency furniture was not, however, only distinguished by its informal arrangement and by its array of styles. Certain pieces and designs became intimately associated with the period by nature of their technological or stylistic innovation or their daring simplicity. One of the most characteristic items in the Regency interior, for example, was the circular, oval, or octagonal table with a simple, single central support. In 1807 Southey recorded that 'our breakfast table is oval, large enough for eight or nine persons, yet supported upon one claw in the centre', adding that 'this is the newest fashion'. By the 1830s these tables were commonplace, and often supported on cast-iron pillars, terminating in a castor (which, in best Regency fashion, was invariably supported by an animal-claw foot). Loudon illustrated one such example in his *Encyclopaedia* of 1833, commenting that 'where the parlour is square, a round table will be found the handsomest and most appropriate piece of furniture'. For larger families or groupings, the Regency solution was the four-legged, D-ended table which could, by the insertion of the requisite number of sections, be expanded so as to fill the

Opposite: A marvellously robust piece of fine, utilitarian Regency furniture from Pickford's House in Friar Gate, Derby. Note the reeded mouldings and paterae.

A Sheraton design for a 'Duchesse' bed. As furniture historian Ralph Fastnedge has remarked, 'The extravagant designs for beds given by Sheraton in the Drawing Book are not representative of the output from the shops.'

room. In 1800 Richard Gillow patented movable sliders of wood or metal which could support the table flaps, thus inaugurating the age of the expandable dining or board-room table.

Equally characteristic of the style and innovation of the Regency was the 'Grecian sofa', which did as much as any single item to transform the appearance of the average drawing room. The couch itself was in origin a form of day-bed; its descendant, the sofa, was distinguished from the settee, which remained an extension of the armchair both in form and in the manner in which it was decorated or upholstered. During the Regency, however, the terms 'sofa' and 'settee' were often interchangeable. There was also the '*tête-à-tête*' – a long seat for two which Karin Walton has found referred to as early as 1792; by 1840 it had evolved into the well-known S-shaped lovers' seat.

Developed from the one-ended couch, the sofa had two, generally scrolled ends of equal height, each of which was invariably provided with a bolster – stuffed with feathers and often decorated with a tassel. It was also usually provided with a good many loose cushions – a characteristic motif of Regency interiors. The sofa first appeared in Sheraton's *Cabinet Dictionary* of 1803 and by the 1820s was seen in most houses of any pretension. 'No parlour is complete without one', claimed Loudon, who suggested that they be stuffed with hair or wool (or, for those with fewer financial resources, hay or straw, or even bran or 'sea wrack grass'), covered with moreen, damask, or black horsehair, fixed with brass nails, and provided with loose covers of glazed or unglazed calico. Ottomans were similar to sofas, but had no visible woodwork; by 1792 they were popular enough to be bought by the Prince of Wales for Carlton House. For all variants of the sofa, sprung upholstery had, by the 1830s, begun to replace the traditional hair or down stuffings.

The sofa also quickly metamorphosed into the sofa-bed. By the 1820s Ackermann was illustrating a number of 'French' sofa-beds, their draperies falling in a rather alarming fashion from the precarious dome above. Not all sofa-beds were as grand as this, however; in his *Encyclopaedia* Loudon illustrated many utilitarian examples which differ little from the basic models available today. To accompany the sofa was another Regency invention: the sofa-table. This piece – which, through the invention of effective oil lamps, could now be used throughout the whole day – served a number of purposes: writing, sewing, reading, and so on; as a result it was predictably promoted as the ideal workmate for the housewife.

Another piece of furniture highly redolent of the Regency in terms of style, innovation, and political quotation was the 'Trafalgar' chair. Variations of this graceful chair, with its elaborate front legs, swept 'sabre' rear legs, curving back, cane seat, and loose squab cushion, could be found in many well-to-do Regency homes – where, Ackermann noted, they were often used in dining rooms, upholstered in red fabric or leather. The name does not come directly from Nelson's victory but probably, reckons furniture historian Clifford Musgrave, from the Trafalgar Workshops of the chairmakers

This attractive giltwood chaise-longue, a one-ended variant of the sofa, epitomizes the seat furniture of the early nineteenth century, with its graceful, sweeping lines, prominent animal motifs and boldly-coloured blue and yellow striped silk upholstery.

Right: Detail of the Grecian sofa from the South Drawing Room at Sir John Soane's Museum. In a yellow to match the walls, with the bolster trimmed in black – a common late Regency device.

Two chaise-longues, illustrated by Ackermann in 1826.

Opposite: Designs by George Smith for a variety of Regency scrolled sofa ends.

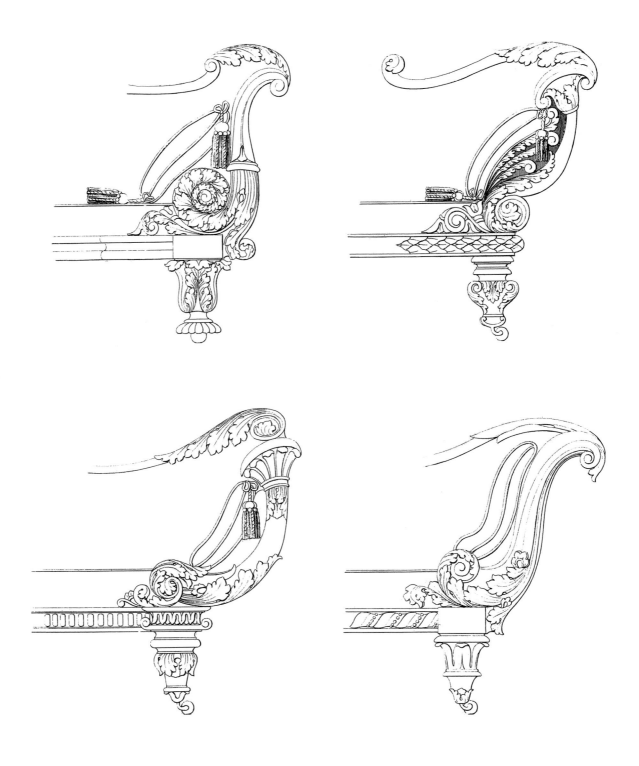

Morgan and Sanders. To cement the tenuous link with the British navy and
with Nelson, however, Trafalgar chairs were often provided with mouldings
in the shape of ropes or cables.

Equally characteristic of the period was the arc-backed 'curule' chair, a
form allegedly taken directly from ancient Greek and Roman models. Many
were given cross-framed legs – a device more usually associated with Regency
stools. Not only were these chairs graceful, clean-lined, and appropriately
antique; their unfussy simplicity and solidity also suggested restful repose. In
1828 Walter Scott wrote that while a chair 'of twenty or thirty years since
was mounted on four tapering and tottering legs, resembling four tobacco-
pipes', modern chairs of this type 'have a curule air, curve outwards behind,
and give a comfortable air of stability to the weighty aristocrat or ponderous
burgess'. Thus were style and fashion cleverly allied to comfort and
practicality, in typical Regency manner. A similar combination was to be
found in the new spoon-back or 'curricle' chairs (the latter name being
coined by Sheraton on account of their resemblance to the small carriages of
the day). These were usually intended for libraries or drawing rooms, where
relaxation was more important than mere show, and were invariably well
upholstered – most probably in the new 'French' fashion, with neat piped,
squared edges more suited to the severe lines of Neo-Classical furniture.

Comfort was indeed one of the major – and most innovative –
prerequisites for the Regency interior. As Karin Walton has noted:
'Lounging is a nineteenth-century concept and was not generally acceptable
in polite eighteenth-century society.' 'Lounging chairs' have been detected as
early as 1802: the accounts for Stourhead in Wiltshire show a bill for '2
Lounging Chairs with sattin wood feet stuffed in fine linens and cushions for
the Seats and Backs on castors'.

Not everyone could afford a set of Trafalgar, curricle, or lounging library
chairs. But even in the humblest homes, new models of stylish yet practical
Regency furniture could be found. 'Windsor' chairs first appeared in about
1810. (Rather confusingly, they actually originated in the Chiltern furniture-
making town of High Wycombe, rather than in the nearby royal seat of
Windsor; no doubt, though, the name was a cunning marketing ploy to
associate these chairs with the great Princely patron himself.) In a few years
they were to be found in kitchens and bedrooms of all descriptions on both
sides of the Atlantic. Their distinctive and instantly recognizable shape – the
hard wooden seat, the arms and the sweeping back rail made in a single piece
– made them a classic item whose success endures today.

*Common Regency chair forms;
top: a caned beechwood chair,
with plain, architectural lines,
of c.1800; middle: a painted
'klismos' chair of c.1810;
bottom: a late eighteenth-
century Windsor chair.*

As new forms of chairs proliferated, so did new types of beds. There
were 'French' beds in the modern vein; canopy or tent beds ('in universal
use', declared Loudon in 1833); four-posters; half-tester beds, which could
even be folded up against the wall; Sheraton's 'Duchess beds', which could be
taken to pieces to form two sofas and a couch; sofa-beds; camp beds; and
countless other varieties.

Mirrors, too, could be found in a wide variety of forms: freestanding,

This Rowlandson cartoon neatly sums up the new importance of lounging in comfort in the Regency interior. Its title is 'My Dog and Me'.

Below, left: A distinctive mahogany Regency armchair, with sabre legs, padded horizontal splat, red velvet upholstery, scrolled arms and unusual twisted and turned back-rail.

Below, right: Even more characteristic of early nineteenth-century design is this ebonized chair with curved back-rails and cross-framed supports. The upholstery is of green velvet.

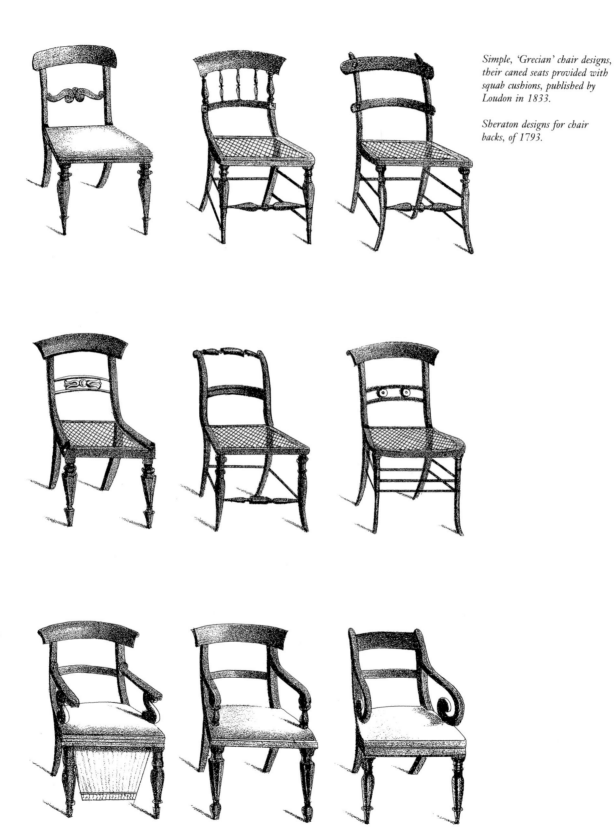

Simple, 'Grecian' chair designs, their caned seats provided with squab cushions, published by Loudon in 1833.

Sheraton designs for chair backs, of 1793.

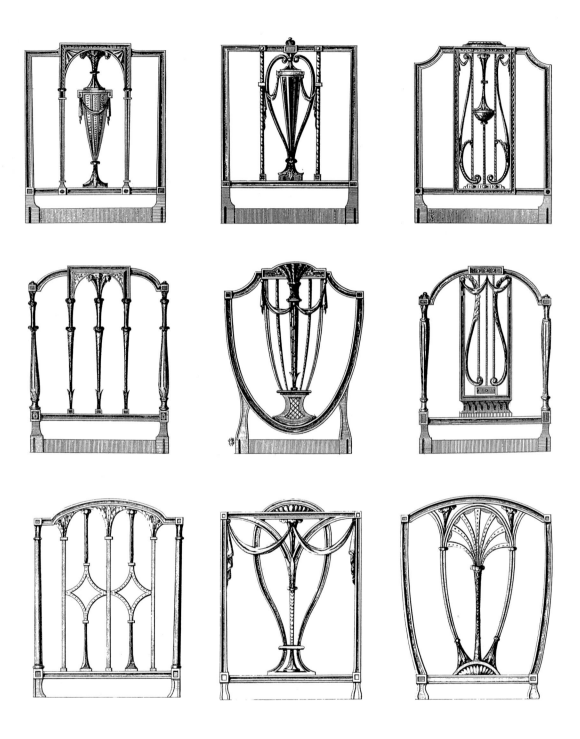

Restrained armchairs and a
characteristically reticent
circular table dominate this
Regency interior at Pitshanger
Manor, west London.

four-footed cheval glasses ('now generally introduced in the sleeping
appartments and dressing rooms of our nobility and persons of distinction',
noted Ackermann in 1827); large, single or tripartite mirrors topped with
Neo-Classical or, later, Gothic ornament; and the new, highly fashionable
circular, convex mirrors – which first appeared from France in 1795 and
which Sheraton lauded in 1803 for the 'agreeable effect' they had 'on the
perspective of the room in which they are suspended'.

More unusual items of furniture were invented, too. Indeed, the Regency
witnessed a craze for the most novel, exotic, and technologically impressive
furniture that could be devised. Regency house owners delighted in the
wonders of the metamorphic chair – which, as Ackermann described it, was
'as firm, safe and solid as a rock, and may, with the greatest ease, by merely
lifting up with the right hand the back of the chair, be metamorphosed into
as complete an arm-chair as can be wished for.'

As metamorphic chairs were the ancestors of the modern recliner, so
'gouty chairs' were the precursors of the modern wheelchair. There was also
other exotica on regular display. 'What-nots' – small stands with shelves;
revolving, circular bookstands; 'moving libraries' – bookcases on castors, first
invented by Gillows in 1811; work-tables concealed in globes; nests of tables
(by no means an invention of the space-conscious twentieth century); and
chiffoniers, the form and identity of which seemed to vary but which were
usually types of commode or sideboard with open shelves. Southey aptly
ridiculed the mania for exotic furniture and meaningless nomenclature while
writing in his adopted guise of a Spanish tourist in 1807:

An upholder [upholsterer] just now advertises *Commodes, Console-tables, Ottomans,
Chaiselonges,* and *Chiffoniers*; – what are all these? you ask. I asked the same question,
and could find no person in the house who could answer me; but they are all articles
of the newest fashion, and no doubt will all soon be thought indispensably necessary
in every well furnished house.

While, however, chiffoniers and what-nots have largely disappeared from
the modern interior, one unusual item of Regency furniture has endured: the
pianoforte. In 1787 a patent was granted for the first upright piano (and, in
true Regency fashion, eight years later the first combined piano-bookcase was
patented, too). And by 1833 Loudon was declaring that: 'The pianoforte is
now to be found in one shape or other, in almost every drawing room, from
that of the humble tradesman, to that of the palace.' They also, he added
(presumably without intending the pun), 'harmonize with the general forms
of drawing room furniture better than they ever did before'. This
proliferation of pianos, together with the manufacture of bookcases in every
conceivable shape and form, suggests perhaps that the average Regency
household was rather more culturally inclined than that of today.

Not only were new items of furniture invented by Regency designers.
New materials – or at least old materials in new contexts – were also used to
make them. Traditional, unpainted oak continued to be used by those who

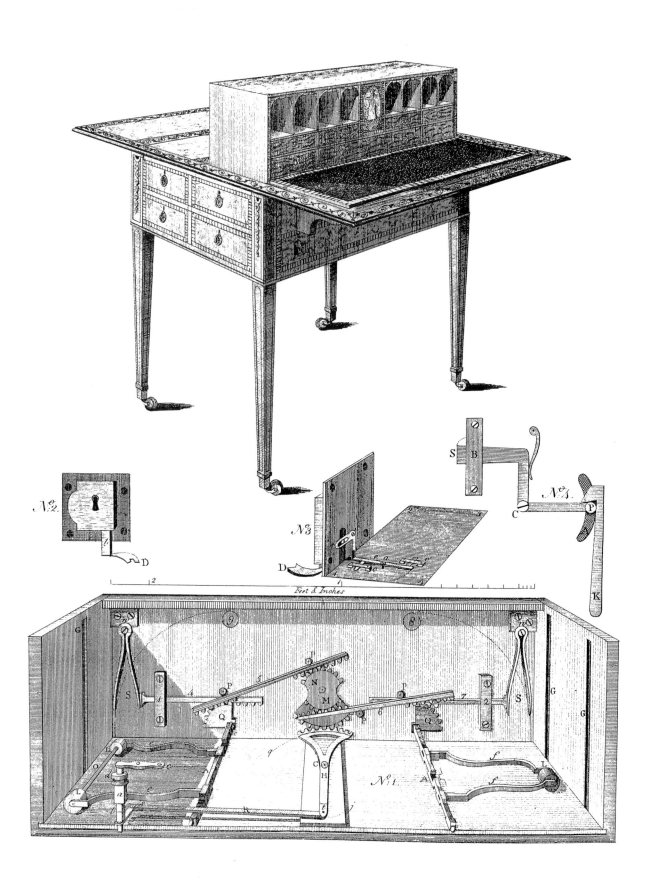

Opposite: A 'Harlequin Pembroke Table', as depicted by Sheraton in 1792, complete with a view of its intriguing mechanism.

Right: An early nineteenth-century ebonized rosewood chiffonier, very much in Hope's heavy 'Egyptian' style. The cupboard door has brass trellis-work and the columns parcel-gilt decoration.

Right, centre: The idea of a nest of tables was not devised by the home entertainers of the 1950s and 60s, but actually first appeared in the pattern-books of Sheraton and his contemporaries. This nest of four tables is made of mahogany with fruitwood banding.

Right, below: The technical wizardry, dual functions and sheer showmanship of metamorphic furniture greatly appealed to Regency householders. Here is a metamorphic mahogany library table of the late eighteenth century, in its alternative guise as a set of library steps.

Far right: A Sheraton design of 1793 for metamorphic library steps.

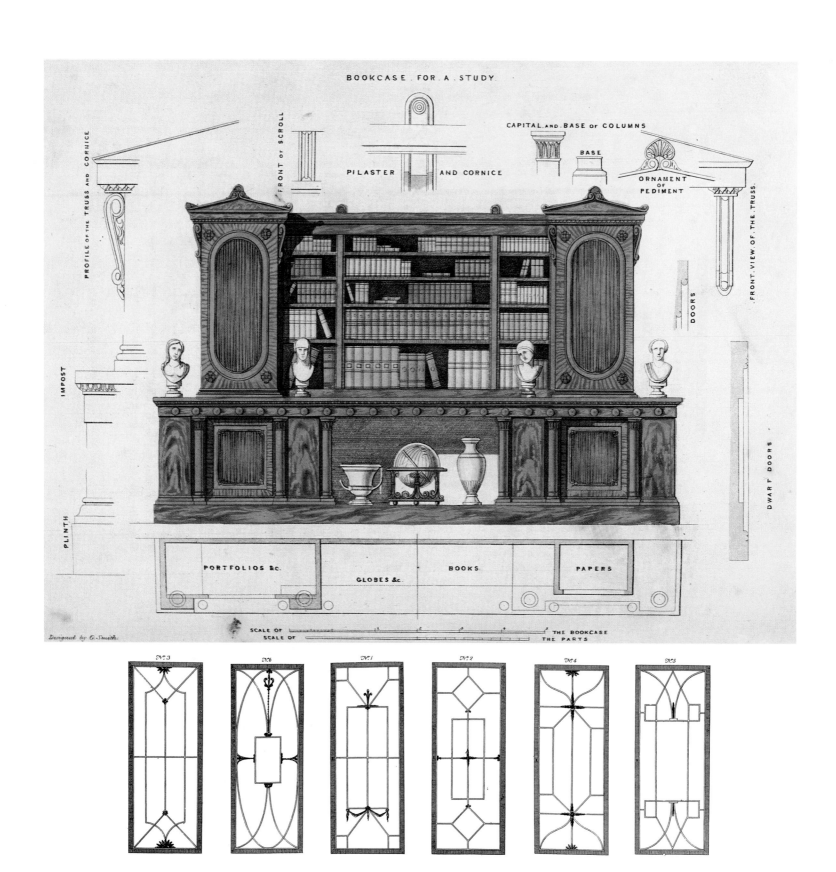

BOOKCASE. FOR. A. STUDY.

The famous movable circular bookcase, as first illustrated by Ackermann in 1810.

Opposite, top: An impressive bookcase design, published by George Smith in 1826.

Opposite, bottom: Glazed bookcase door designs, proffered by Sheraton in 1792.

could afford it – but primarily for the newly fashionable Gothic furniture of the 1820s and 1830s. Alongside oak and mahogany (still especially recommended for drawing rooms and libraries), new, foreign woods were being imported to feed the increasing demand for novelty and colour. Rosewood and yellow-white satinwood were particularly prevalent in the furniture of the period, as were rarer species such as tulipwood and zebrawood. The great expense of the latter effectively confined it to veneers or to stringing work; even then, however, Maria Edgeworth complained in 1820 that supplies of zebrawood were almost exhausted and that there was 'no more of it to be had for love nor money'.

Wood was not the only material utilized for furniture. Heavy hall or garden chairs, which were largely sedentary, were beginning to be made not of traditional hard or softwoods but of cast iron, as Loudon explained in 1833: 'Lobby chairs, being seldom moved, may be made of heavy massive forms in timber, or of cast iron, so as to have a decidedly architectural character.' Lead was frequently used for cast or stamped applied decoration, as was brass, the most common metal for furniture handles and knobs. (That characteristically Regency item, the lion's-head brass furniture handle, first appeared around 1800.) Marble, too, was being revived as a material for table-tops – particularly marble from British quarries, so enthusiastically recommended by Ackermann and his contemporaries.

While expensive woods such as mahogany or rosewood were left unadorned, most of the cheaper furniture woods were painted or stained during the Regency period – much as panelling, when of pine, fir, or beech, was always painted. The most common paint treatment was graining, which was held to be particularly appropriate for 'oaken' Gothic furniture. Loudon recommended that hall chairs be grained – or, interestingly, 'painted the colour of the wall against which it is to stand', a practice which does not always correspond with modern ideas of interior decoration. Alternatively, chairs or tables could be bronzed, that is, painted green in imitation of patinated antique bronze, and possibly given a dusting of a bronze-coloured metal powder for added effect.

Furniture painting did not merely involve the application of one flat colour. Beech was frequently painted in imitation of bamboo – with shadows, joints, and knots where appropriate. And Classical scenes or architectural motifs were often painted onto chair backs, especially in bedrooms or drawing rooms. Bedrooms, being more 'feminine' in function and tone (or so the designers of the time reckoned), were held to be a most suitable setting for painted pieces. Jane Austen's mysterious, locked bedroom in *Northanger Abbey* was revealed to contain 'neatly painted chairs'; indeed, in *Pride and Prejudice* Charles Bingley flatly declared that in his experience women 'all paint tables, cover screens, and net purses'.

To achieve a more realistic impression of fine woods such as oak or rosewood, furniture could be stained rather than painted. The intention was, as with so much of the Regency home, to suggest grander materials and thus

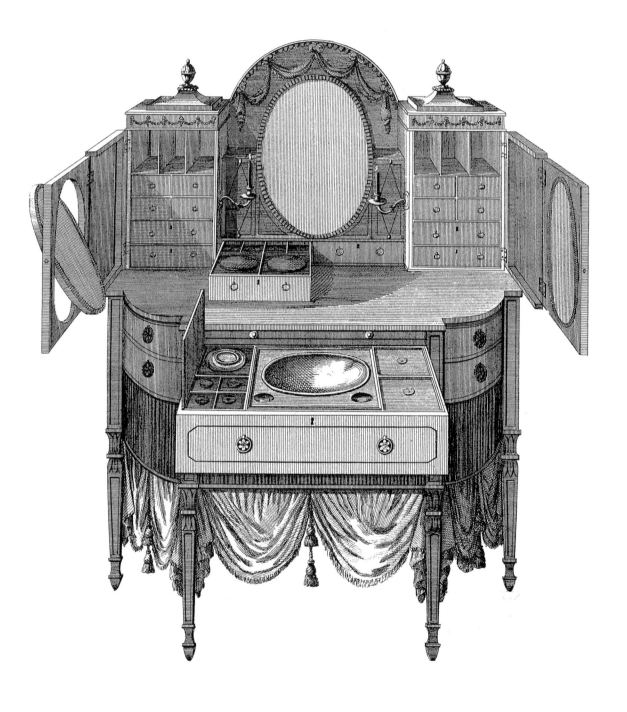

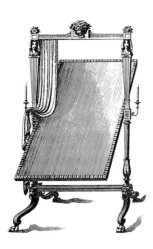

Above and right: Sheraton mirrors: two cheval glasses, and (far right) a combined dressing glass and writing table.

Right, below: This fascinating design for a 'Bidet Dressing Table' was published by Sheraton in 1793. Complete with 'Night Table' it provided a wide range of facilities for day- and night-time use.

Opposite: Sheraton's 'Lady's Cabinet Dressing Table' includes all the fittings that any woman of fashion could wish for.

greater wealth. Chairs of the 1820s and 1830s were often stained pink in an effort to reproduce the colour of rosewood, yellow for seasoned oak, or red for West Indian mahogany. Hay, Loudon, and other late Regency writers gave numerous formulae and procedures for such operations. Loudon suggested staining beech Windsor chairs 'with diluted sulphuric acid and logwood' to attain a red, mahogany hue – or, less pleasantly, with 'quicklime slaked in urine, and laid on the wood while hot'. Neither of these appear to be a process which it is really worth repeating nowadays.

As already noted, the grandest Regency interiors were rich with gilt, and this included the furniture. This largely French-inspired fashion was given a further boost by Hope's furniture of 1807; two years later Ackermann reported that the very Hope-inspired decorative scheme of 'black chairs, ornamented with metal gilt, in various elegant devices, are in universal use'. Ackermann also observed that gilt used in combination with brass or bronzing 'still continues in use in the more ornamental and decorative articles of tables, candelabras, glasses, and cornices for windows'. Mirror and picture frames were invariably gilded; Loudon condemned the old practice of covering frames with velvet or a similar rich material, as such fabrics soiled easily. The *Repository* strongly promoted the idea that all decorative features should be gilt or gold-coloured; even fabrics should always be provided with gold borders or tassels of 'gold-coloured silk'.

More expensive still were the decorative finishes of 'verre églomisé' – engraved gold leaf under a protective layer of glass – and boulle, the French brass-and-tortoiseshell (or exotic wood) inlay work so beloved by George IV, who had it applied in copious quantities on his furniture at Brighton Pavilion during the 1820s. More accessible to the average purse was a 'japan' finish for furniture – red, green, but predominantly black in colour. By the end of the eighteenth century the application of oriental lacquer – the correct use of the term 'japanning' – was being revived for the first time since the seventeenth century. In 1800 over sixty japanners were listed in London alone. Yet this fashion did not outlive the Regency period: much so-called 'japanning' was merely varnished black paint, instead of countless layers of oriental lacquer – much in the same way that the term 'ormolu' was used to apply not just to gilded metal but to any finish involving lacquered or varnished brass. Even the shimmering metal dust applied to the japanning to give it an expensive-looking, lustrous effect soon fell off. Such cheap, glittering effects were too superficial for the sober world of Victorian England, and by 1840 the technique was dead.

The architect Thomas Hopper held that 'it is an architect's business to understand all styles, and to be prejudiced in favour of none'. One of the many stylistic approaches he pioneered was the short-lived Norman Revival, seen opposite in the Ebony Room at Penrhyn Castle in Wales, begun in 1825. The heaviness of neo-Norman forms such as these, however, ensured that this particular style did not win many admirers.

NOW HERE IS THE SAME PLACE CORRECTED – TRIMMED – POLISHED – DECORATED – ADORNED. HERE SWEEPS A PLANTATION, IN THAT BEAUTIFUL REGULAR CURVE: THERE WINDS A GRAVEL WALK . . . HERE A LARCH, THERE A LILAC; HERE A RHODODENDRON, THERE AN ARBUTUS. THE STREAM, YOU SEE, IS BECOME A CANAL: THE BANKS ARE PERFECTLY SMOOTH AND GREEN, SLOPING TO THE WATER'S EDGE: AND THERE IS LORD LITTLEBRAIN, ROWING IN AN ELEGANT BOAT.

(THOMAS PEACOCK,
Headlong Hall, 1816)

*A cast-iron verandah of 1810
with typical anthemion motifs
at Nanhoron, north Wales.
Technology and nature simply
combined in the best Regency
manner.*

No examination of the style and form of the Regency home can be complete without a look at the Regency garden. For as this period developed, house and garden became increasingly integrated, until by the 1820s the garden was virtually regarded as an organic extension of the drawing room.

The aspect of the Regency garden, like that of the house it enclosed, was considerably altered not only by technological advances but also by philosophical developments. The early Georgians had revolted against the formalism of the French to produce the new 'English Garden'; whereas, however, this style was much admired for its freedom and naturalism, its planned landscapes were in reality anything but natural. The 1780s in turn witnessed a strong reaction against these contrived 'improvements' which, as designed by Capability Brown and his followers, so dominated the mid-eighteenth-century rural landscape. The poet William Cowper was at the forefront of the attacks on the 'improvers'. In place of Brown's elaborately arranged parks, he advocated a humble deference to nature, based firmly on the precept that 'God made the country and man made the town'. To him

Capability Brown and his acolytes were tampering with God's creation:

Improvement, the idol of the age,
Is fed with many a victim. Lo! He comes, –
The omnipotent magician, Brown, appears . . .
He speaks. The lake in front becomes a lawn,
Woods vanish, hills subside, and vallies rise . . .

Cowper's devotion to the principle of unsullied Nature formed the basis of the early Regency landscape as interpreted by practitioners such as Humphry Repton and Uvedale Price; however, the theoretical clarity of Cowper's naturalistic ideal was soon adapted by these men to be compatible with more sophisticated tastes. Repton launched himself as a professional gardener and landscape designer in 1788 and was soon being acclaimed the leading designer of the age. His primary interest, however, was in large-scale landscapes, in which he could realize his grand vision of the 'picturesque principle' – the creation of an open-air composition which would parallel the somewhat staged, Arcadian visions of the seventeenth-century French painters Claude and Poussin.

The fact that such painterly idylls actually more resembled Marie Antoinette's naïve frolics in the gardens at Versailles than the true state of the British countryside was, however, quickly grasped. In 1805 Joseph Gandy broke with the picturesque movement and called for a new, realistic and utilitarian approach to garden design, one that would benefit the most humble suburban terrace as well as the great parks of the mighty landowners. Gandy's opponents were quick to label this approach 'frigid', but its emphasis on convenience and neatness, rather than on the vague, poetic ideals of the picturesque, had much more popular appeal to middle-class families who were seeking merely to enlist nature to soften the aspect of their immediate architectural and urban environments. Most importantly, this thesis was as appropriate to the small cottage or terrace garden as to the great estate. Landscape theory had finally come to the modest garden; and in 1803 this theory found a new champion – a landscape gardener who, while only twenty years old when he came south from Scotland to set up practice, rapidly came to dominate the development of the Regency garden: John Claudius Loudon.

One of the most striking and frequently expressed sentiments in Loudon's many published works on gardens was the emphasis on the primacy of nature, even at the expense of the architecture of the house. In 1823 Papworth noted the change of emphasis: whereas 'it was the practice formerly to exhibit the house, as standing alone in the cube-formed nakedness of its construction' and 'no tree was permitted to interrupt the prospect of the house itself', 'in new creations the architect considers the house . . . and the plantations as a great whole'.

This fashion was encouraged by the passion of the 1790s for romantic Gothic novels, with their murky backgrounds, their thick woods, and their rustling vegetation. Jane Austen, too, (who so expertly satirized the Gothic

novel in *Northanger Abbey*) decried those who sought to 'improve' nature: in
Pride and Prejudice (written in 1797, published in 1813), Darcy's mansion was
eulogized by a rapt Elizabeth, who 'had never seen a place for which nature
had done more, or where natural beauty had been so little counteracted by
an awkward taste'. Even Repton – more used to landscaping estates than
designing urban gardens – was by no means immune to the lure of the
climbing creeper and the masking conifer. At Sezincote in 1805 he was
careful to soften the lines of Cockerell's marvellous 'Indian' mansion by
arranging trees and shrubs both alongside and clinging to the masonry.

For the first time the house was now being seen as an integral part of the
garden, and vice versa. No longer were the interior and exterior of the family
home to be kept at arm's length from flower and vegetable planting. The
emphasis on placing all of the main rooms at ground-floor level – and not, as
formerly, on the first floor – together with the provision of, as Papworth
noted, propped-open 'casements that descend to the very floor', gave 'ready
access at all times' to the natural beauties outside. Loudon strongly suggested
that 'the Flower-garden should generally adjoin the conservatory, or at all
events be connected with it by a verandah, colonnade, arcade, or covered way
of some description', while Papworth welcomed the trend to bring the
greenhouse 'from its heretofore distant station' to abut the principal rooms.

By 1840 villa, cottage, and even urban terrace gardens were seen as
natural, verdant extensions of the brickwork and stucco. The verandah
rapidly became popular after *c.*1790: sometimes glazed, usually provided with
lively ironwork, it was invariably festooned with honeysuckles (one of the
most popular plants of the period), wistaria, Virginia creeper, ivy, or other
climbers, all of which were enjoying a huge vogue. Larger plants were
deployed to mask the rigid lines of wall and window, too. 'Trees improve the
outline of most buildings' advised Loudon in 1838, and he urged that, in
order to provide longer-lasting cover for adjacent masonry, masking trees and
shrubs should be of the evergreen variety – possibly one of the many species
now being imported from North America.

William Wordsworth was keen to embrace this celebration of nature, in
his garden as well as in his verse. He relished the prospect of buildings
appearing to grow out of their natural surroundings, with man as an
interested but powerless observer. At his own home at Rydal Mount in
Cumbria he put these theories into practice in the years after 1813,
developing his garden in a manner which eschewed rigid planning or
improvement and which provided Dorothy and himself with rapid access to
their beloved fells. Loudon regarded Rydal Mount as one of the few 'very
perfect' residences in the north, and its lack of pretension and formality
proved a substantial influence on his subsequent works.

Not everyone could afford a rural paradise such as Rydal Mount; yet
even the smallest and humblest garden could be transformed by the new
philosophy. One particularly marked development in gardens of all sizes was
the new provision of grass lawns. Large areas of grass were widespread in

The back garden of a modest house belonging to the Pole family in King Square, Bristol, in a view of c.1806. The broad, gravelled walk runs the whole length of the garden, and is bordered by narrow flower-beds and high, creeper-covered walls.

The 'potting house' in the Poles garden in King Square, Bristol.

gardens by 1810, and no doubt completely transformed the urban landscape. Maintaining them, however, was no easy task: the modern cylinder lawnmower was invented by Edwin Budding in 1830, but it was twenty years before it had truly caught on, and in the meantime lawns had to be painstakingly manicured by more laborious means.

Grass was by no means ubiquitous, however, and there were still more areas covered with hard surfaces than is common in gardens today. Loudon's 'architectural gardens' were paved with flagstones and set about with urns and statues. More commonly, paths of gravel – or if this could not be afforded, sand or even coal-ash – were arranged about the rear garden. Gravel paths frequently surrounded the garden, allowing for a pleasant walk after dinner; paths also wound across the lawns in serpentine fashion – a subtle nod in the direction of the picturesque. In his *Encyclopaedia of Gardening* of 1822 Loudon enthused over the prospect of fragrant camomile pathways but, more realistically, advised that 'grass walks may do' only where 'gravel is scarce'. At the same time, sinuous paths were all very well, but in smaller gardens they should always be put to some distinct purpose. 'A walk should always proceed', Loudon declared, 'from the main entrance to the main object of the garden.' Views from these paths were meant to vary constantly; the paths themselves, though, were never meant to be part of these attractive vignettes and were often hidden by dwarf box borders, by shrubs, or even by low stone walls. In 1823 this rule was included in Papworth's checklist of requirements for garden paths: they 'should not be viewed from the windows' and 'should not be seen to cross the lawn'; they 'should not seem to divide portions of lawn or shrubbery into equal parts'; they 'should not be quickly sinuous without sufficient cause'; parallel paths should be avoided; and grass walks should be wide enough 'that the footstep may not be constrained to form a beaten-path'.

Grass was not only used to transform gardens behind the house. In the last decades of the eighteenth century gardens began to appear for the first time at the *front* of the terrace or villa, as well as the cottage. Unfortunately, most of them have since been built over; yet plans and perspectives of recommended designs for front gardens still survive in contemporary manuals. Front gardens were generally more Spartan and utilitarian in their planning than those at the rear. Possibly the most common form was a large lawn, set perhaps with one or two beds and a small tree or two, and bisected by a straight gravel pathway terminating at the gate.

For those in town and city squares who had insufficient room to accommodate even small front gardens, a strip of private garden was introduced immediately in front of the terrace, between the main road and the public square garden. This device afforded excellent views from first-floor drawing rooms or verandahs; with the road invisible immediately below, the impression could be gained that all the verdant terrain you looked out upon – both the private garden and the public square beyond – was your own property.

Brick paviors form the garden walks at Ash-Lawn Highland, Virginia. James Monroe – later Fifth President of the United States – bought this plot, adjacent to his friend Thomas Jefferson, in 1793, and lived here until 1823. The garden still retains its quiet, Federal charm.

Below: A Coade Stone pedestal – a common ornament in larger Regency gardens. This sort of delightful garden statuary is now much at risk from architectural theft.

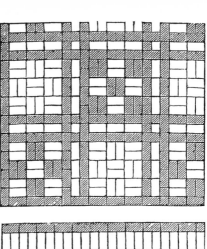

Right: Ornamental garden urns of the 1830s, drawn by J. C. Loudon. All of these were, Loudon emphasized, made not of stone or of plaster but of 'Austin's artificial stone' – a hard-wearing ceramic, very like Coade Stone, which was ideal for garden ornaments.

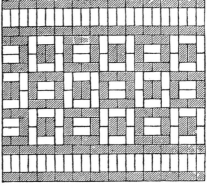

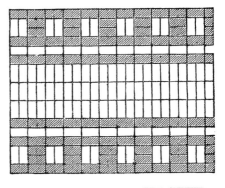

Far right: Tessellated garden pavement designs, from Loudon's Encyclopaedia.

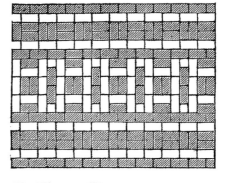

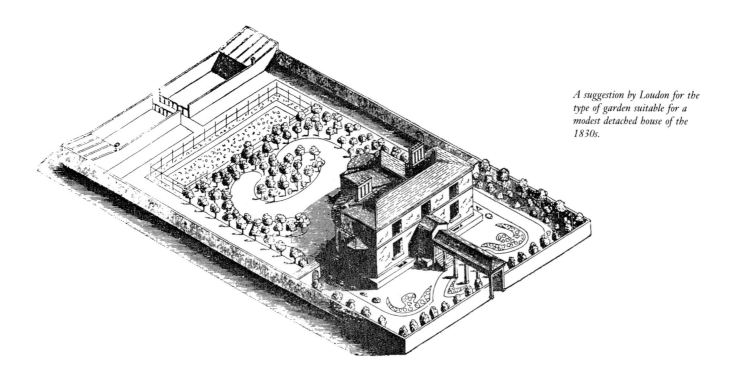

A suggestion by Loudon for the type of garden suitable for a modest detached house of the 1830s.

Gardens devised by Loudon for a pair of semi-detached, Fourth Rate homes: left, a radical, geometric design; opposite, a more conventional layout.

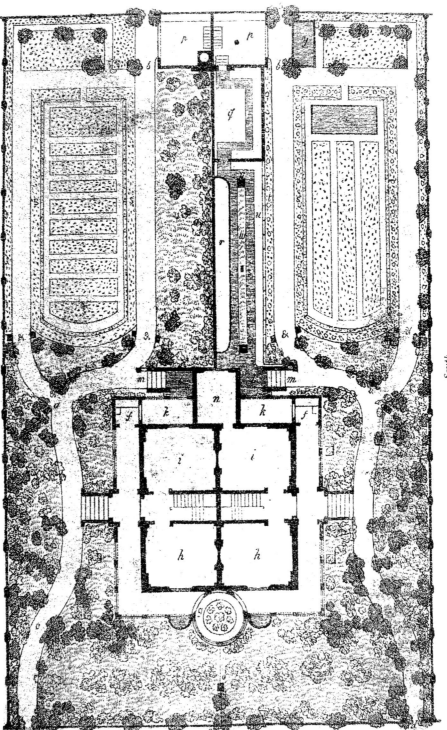

South.

Particularly fashionable during the Regency period was the stylish, flower-strewn 'botanic garden'. Beds in both front and rear gardens were not of the regular, right-angled variety so beloved of modern municipal planters. They could be of any exotic shape: oval, diamond, star, circle, crescent, teardrop – anything but a square or rectangle. A new emphasis was placed on mingling flower colours, in contrast to the traditional preference for single-species beds. At the same time, evergreens and climbers were enthusiastically recommended to break up the horizontal and vertical lines. These varieties proved particularly useful for urban gardens, where the flora had to be strong enough to survive the smoke and associated effluvia of the new industrial age. Loudon himself was especially fond of evergreen shrubs such as rhododendrons and variegated holly; the result of this enthusiasm is that rhododendrons have reproduced to become almost a weed in many parts of the country. Interestingly, many of these hardy shrubs were not indigenous but came from across the Atlantic. In 1822, for example, Loudon noted that 'it is only since the recent great influx of trees and shrubs from America' that 'the idea of arranging shrubs' had become widespread.

Garden walls were not so much affected by changes in fashion and taste as by technological improvements. All the leading garden designers of the period expressed their abhorrence of obstructive and unnaturally high brick walls, preferring fences which were as invisible as possible – low, of wicker, chains, or better still, iron railings painted dark green. Repton's opinion of fences was that 'it is hardly necessary to say, that the less they are seen the better; and therefore a dark, or as it is called, an invisible green . . . is the proper colour'. This use of green was extended to gates and indeed to all other items of garden furniture. In his *Pickwick Papers* of 1836–7, Dickens sagely observed of Sam Weller's front garden that 'in many parts of the world, men do come out of gardens, close green gates after them, and even walk briskly away, without attracting any particular share of public observation.'

Unsubtle and obtrusive fencing was a particular bugbear of Loudon's. 'It is not uncommon, in the suburbs of London', he lamented in his *Suburban Gardener* of 1838, 'to find a fence in a straight line, and parallel to it a serpentine gravel walk.' Rear walls were often flued to allow for internal heating, enabling more exotic tropical plants to be grown alongside the brickwork. In 1822 Loudon noted that 'there are very generally flued walls in all modern gardens north of London' – which rather implies that the south was shamefully backward in terms of garden technology. Such walls were heated either by smoke from traditional coal or wood fires set into the wall, or alternatively by the new instruments of industrial power – steam or hot water. In larger gardens, cross walls as well as boundary walls may have been flued, creating an almost sub-tropical atmosphere where desired. These brick walls were on occasion colour-washed white or black – the latter being generally preferred for 'absorbing and radiating more heat than any other, and thereby accelerating the maturity, and improving the quality of fruits'.

*Above: Humphry Repton's view
of how the immediate landscape
could be improved through the
judicious use of 'invisible'
garden fencing.*

*Right: 'Invisible' fences from
J. B. Papworth's beautifully
illustrated* Hints on
Ornamental Gardening *of
1823.*

*Looking into the library from
the conservatory at Thomas
Hope's Deepdene, Surrey, in a
watercolour of 1823. This view
illustrates well the effortless
blending of nature and
architecture so sought after in
the Regency home.*

Top: One of the first constructions to make use of the new, curved iron glazing bar: the conservatory at Grove House, Regent's Park, London, of 1823. In November of that year the architect C. R. Cockerell visited the newly-erected conservatory and noted that it 'has an elegant form but looks as fragile as blubber'.

Bottom: The Palm-House of 1825 at Bicton Park, Devon. Probably designed by the architects Decimus Burton and George Webster, who were responsible for the similarly curvilinear conservatory of 1826 at Dallam Tower in Cumbria.

Flued walls were not, however, sufficient to help propagate the species being discovered with increasing frequency in the remote corners of the world. For this a greenhouse was needed, and it was the rapid metamorphosis of the greenhouse or conservatory which provided the most dramatic development of the Regency garden. And unsurprisingly, Loudon was at the forefront. In 1815 Sir George Mackenzie published an article calling for the introduction of glass greenhouse roofs 'parallel to the vaulted surface of the heavens, or to the plane of the sun's orbit', which included a design for a revolutionary greenhouse built as a half-dome and not as the habitual straight-sided glass box. The following year Loudon patented the curved cast-iron glazing bar for specific use in greenhouses. The effect of this invention was substantial, enabling Mackenzie's vision to be promptly realized.

No longer did greenhouses have to resemble flat-walled houses; instead, new curved-roof greenhouses – most effective when built as a complete hemisphere – could present a far larger area for the sun to shine through, and thus proved far more effective at propagation. In 1823 Loudon erected a domed conservatory on the side of his own villa in Porchester Terrace, in the fashionable Bayswater area of west London, and was soon enthusing about its properties and advantages:

The greenhouse may be designed in any form, and placed in almost any situation . . . Even a house looking due north, if glazed on three sides of the roof, will preserve plants in a healthy, vigorous state. The curvilinear principle applied to this class of structures admits of every combination of form . . . [and soon] the clumsy shed-like wooden or mixed roofs now in use will be erected only in nursery and market gardens.

The progression from wood to metal glazing bars of iron or even copper was, as garden historian Melanie Simo has noted, 'the greatest improvement hitherto made in horticultural architecture'. Metal-framed glasshouses were provided with another recent advance: steam heating, supplied through cast-iron piping. This combination of greenhouse and steam was first attempted in 1788 and by 1820 was widespread. Most importantly, this stylish adornment to the house and garden was within reach of every class of household. As Loudon pompously noted in 1838, 'the enjoyments afforded by a greenhouse, however small, are very considerable; and where there are children, these enjoyments may be mingled with useful instruction.'

Over thirty years earlier Loudon had recommended gardening as a suitable pastime for bored housewives ('The study of Botany is certainly', he claimed, 'peculiarly calculated for ladies'). More significantly, Prince Pückler-Muskau suggested that women were largely responsible for the revival of flower gardening in the 1810s and 1820s. (Loudon was, however, careful to add the caveat that 'where the mistress of the house has not a taste for plants' and 'no gardener is kept; the greenhouse is in danger of becoming a nuisance'.) The conservatory remained first and foremost an area for the

Left: *A view of the interior of Thomas Hopper's eccentric Gothic Conservatory at Carlton House, built in 1807 but demolished only twenty years later. The top-lighting was particularly impressive. However, the building leaked badly; in 1822 Nash reported that the glazed vaulting was 'worse than useless as a roof', and recommended replacing it with plaster. When it was demolished the grand armorial glass in the windows and the unusual Coade Stone candelabra were sent to Windsor Castle.*

Below: *The clean, architectural geometry of this Papworth-designed greenhouse gives it a very modern air.*

Green House

whole family, to be used not only for horticultural study but as a drawing room, or even as an especially pleasant breakfast room – 'which', declared Loudon, 'ought to embrace the morning sun, and invite [one] to go abroad'.

As today, the most suitable form for the Regency conservatory or greenhouse (there was no distinction made between the two terms; the former was simply more pretentious) was obviously that which best harmonized with the adjoining house. Unfortunately, although modern Britain is currently enjoying a revival of interest in conservatories, many manufacturers appear to have forgotten this simple precept, and their designs have degenerated into crude, over-sized parodies of Regency or Victorian models. Size is often a particular problem; yet during the 1820s advances in cast-iron construction had made the production of even the smallest conservatories wholly economic. 'There can be no reason', declared Loudon's hugely successful *Encyclopaedia* of 1833, 'why a small house should not have a large conservatory.' Loudon actually recommended dismantling smaller conservatories in the summer months and reusing the glass and iron panels as cold-frames for delicate blooms.

By 1830 metal-and-glass conservatories of every size could be found all over Britain. At Carlton House the Regent himself had installed a vast Gothic structure, records of which now, alas, survive only in the pages of Pyne's *Royal Residences*. And in 1836 work began on perhaps the most famous private greenhouse of all. The 'Great Stove' at Chatsworth in Derbyshire was 277 feet long and 123 feet wide, and provision was made to enable a coach-and-four to be driven with ease through the middle. Sadly, however, this testimony to Regency glasshouse design is gone too, inexplicably demolished in 1920.

To furnish these new conservatories were countless newly discovered plants. As soldiers and diplomats extended the influence of the British Crown – and, of course, of the East India Company – into yet more far-flung territories, they brought back with them many of the rare and exotic blooms they found there. These could now be safely accommodated not just at the Royal Horticultural Society's gardens at Kew but in any average, heated greenhouse. While the British were building their grand governmental retreat at Simla in the Indian Himalayas, inquisitive and energetic officials, exploring the nearby terrain more extensively, were rewarded with the discovery of a wide variety of unusual and colourful flora and fauna. The wild strawberry was brought back from the Himalayas in 1804 and swiftly became a favourite for hanging baskets or ground cover; the oriental fuchsia, too, quickly became a favourite in the greenhouse. Further east, trade with China resulted in the introduction into Britain of the hydrangea (brought back by Joseph Banks in 1808) and possibly the most characteristic flower of the period, the chrysanthemum. Purple chrysanthemum varieties had arrived via France in 1790, but in 1808 Sir Abraham Hume sent back cuttings direct from China; the flower was an instant success, and by 1834 there were fifty recorded varieties of chrysanthemum available. Expanding trade links also

Top: A garden seat, designed by Repton and published by Ackermann in 1822.

Above: A Regency garden seat from Shrubland Hall, Suffolk. The garland is authentic to the period; the pale blue, alas, is not.

Left: Two garden seat designs from J. B. Papworth's delightful Rural Residences of 1818.

George Tod's 'Pinery and Orangery . . . for John Walter, Esqr., of Teddington', from his Plans . . . for Hot Houses and Green Houses of 1807.

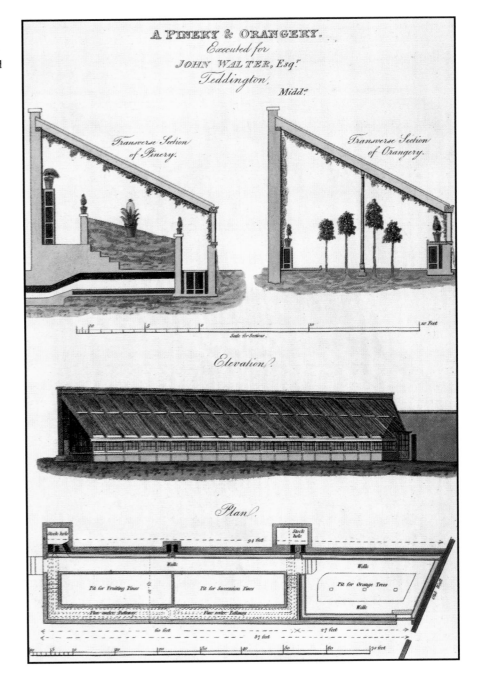

helped foster other new species from the other side of the globe, the petunia and verbena being brought over from South America after the revolutions of the mid-1820s had opened the former Spanish colonies to pragmatic British mercantile influences.

This is not to say, however, that old favourites were neglected. The anemone remained hugely popular, one large nursery listing seventy-five types in 1820. So too was the camellia, a flower much loved by Loudon himself; his *Green-House Companion* of 1824 declared that camellias and geraniums provided 'an inexhaustible fund of beauty . . . for every month of the year', and camellias featured prominently in his own front garden at Bayswater. The rose, of course, was still a perennial favourite; in 1802 the Virginian John Champneys, crossing a musk rose with an imported China rose, effectively invented the modern craze for rose breeding.

Fruit growing, too, was remarkably prevalent and received a further stimulus from the introduction of the heated greenhouse, in which vines and peach, fig, lemon, and orange trees could all be easily grown. Technological advances even provoked a revival in the propagation of the pineapple, the President of the Horticultural Society himself using 'bottom heating' to grow this most architectural and stylish of fruits in 1819. And berry fruits were constantly recommended to serve as borders or terminations for rear gardens of all dimensions.

The conservatory was not, however, the only man-made object permitted in the Regency garden. Movable tubs, pots, and Neo-Classical urns of wood, china, Coade stone, or cast iron were placed about the lawns, beds, and shrubs, sometimes even on walls. Loudon felt that in smaller gardens too many urns or statues would prove a distraction, and such objects should only be used 'very sparingly'.

There was also a marked increase in the provision of garden seating. The Marquis of Blandford had 'barrel seats' made of china placed about his garden, while at Deepdene Thomas Hope installed cedar seats – many in the Gothic style – in 1815. Most gardens, however, had plainer furniture made of wood, wicker or, increasingly, of cast iron. If painted, such furniture was invariably coloured green – *never* white. The modern obsession with using virginal, bleached white for painting garden furniture – and indeed for everything else inside and outside the house – would have appalled Regency Britain, where fashion and taste tended to concur with Repton's severe judgement against 'the garish ostentation of white paint'. Misplaced puritanism was definitely not a concern of the Regency gardener.

Opposite: The Vinery from Repton's Fragment on . . . landscape gardening of 1816.

This is not designed as an exhaustive glossary of every architect and designer of the period, but rather as a biographical summary of those figures who feature in the text of the book. Thus, architects who specialized in grand ecclesiastical or domestic projects, and who had little influence on the development of the average dwelling, are necessarily omitted. For a comprehensive guide to the architects of the period, see Howard Colvin's *Biographical Dictionary of British Architects 1600–1840* (1978); for a similar guide to furniture-makers, see Geoffrey Beard and Christopher Gilbert, eds., *Dictionary of English Furniture Makers 1660–1840* (1986).

ACKERMANN, RUDOLPH (1764–1840)
Born near Leipzig, in 1783 Ackermann came to Paris, and in 1786 to London, where he started in the carriage trade. In 1795 he opened a shop in the Strand, which functioned as an art supplier, publishing house, and drawing school. Between 1809 and 1828 he published *The Repository of the Arts*, a periodical which popularized a number of interior decorating trends. Its range was vast, and in addition to the countless coloured illustrations, the accompanying text was extremely well informed. The *Repository* remained in the vanguard of interior taste for almost twenty years; in 1825, for example, Ackermann kindled the rage for Gothic by publishing A. C. Pugin's plates of Gothic interiors (q.v.).

BALDWIN, THOMAS (1750–1820)
Originally a speculative builder in Bath (an occupation terminated by his bankruptcy in 1793), Baldwin was responsible for the design of some of the most impressive and well-known buildings of Georgian Bath, including the Cross Bath (*c.*1784), Great Pulteney Street (1789), and Bath Street (1791). He also planned neighbouring Bathwick New Town, designing many of the houses there himself.

BULLOCK, GEORGE (*c.*1777–1818)
A designer and craftsman who began as a sculptor but who also later worked as a furniture designer, as an upholsterer, and as an architect. Most famous for his use of British woods and marbles, Bullock owned the Mona Marble Works in Anglesey, and during 1816–17 he supplied Ackermann with many of the plates for the *Repository*. As Beard and Gilbert note, 'Whilst most of his furniture was Neo-Classical in style, some was Gothic, Elizabethan and Jacobean, and he developed these styles far beyond other designers of his day.'

BURTON, DECIMUS (1800–81)
The son of a builder, Burton began practising as an architect at the very early age of nineteen. The architect of many of the buildings in Nash's Regent's Park development (Nash being a close friend of his father's) and of numerous country houses, he is best remembered today as the architect of the screen at Hyde Park Corner (1824–5), the arch on Constitution Hill, by Buckingham Palace (1827–8), and – in collaboration with Joseph Paxton – the famous Great Conservatory erected at Chatsworth during the 1830s.

BUSBY, CHARLES AUGUSTUS (1788–1834)
Busby's early career as an architect was cut short by his bankruptcy in 1814, as a result of the failure of a number of his roofs; this prompted him to flee to America to escape his creditors, whence he returned only in 1820. Although he failed to establish himself in London, he moved to Brighton where he began a partnership with the architect Amon Wilds (q.v.). Busby, as Colvin has noted, 'ranks as one of the principal creators of Regency Brighton'; much of Kemp Town and Brunswick Town, developed by himself and Wilds, was probably built to his design – including the exotic Gothic House on Western Road of *c.*1823.

CHIPPENDALE, THOMAS, the Younger (1749–1822)
The eldest son of a renowned father, he was brought up to run his father's business, which he took over (on Thomas senior's death in 1779) in partnership with Thomas Haig. Haig died hugely in debt in 1803, as a result of which Chippendale was declared bankrupt in 1804. However, he managed to survive this setback, largely since the demand for his furniture – produced to the same high standards of design and craftsmanship as in his father's day – was even greater than when his father had been alive.

COADE, ELEANOR, the Younger (1732–1821)
The daughter of the Eleanor Coade who had founded the Coade Manufactory at Lambeth in 1769, Eleanor joined the firm (which made a particularly hard-wearing form of ceramic, called Coade Stone) and continued to run it after her mother's death. (The Coades were a long-lived family: Mrs Coade senior died in 1796, aged eighty-eight, whilst her daughter lived to be eighty-nine.) As well as manufacturing countless plaques, statues, urns, keystones, and other decorative pieces, the Coade manufactory was most renowned during the Regency period for the gigantic Coade model of a West Indiaman, erected over the entrance to London's West India Docks in 1804, and for Exeter Cathedral's deceptive Coade west window of 1810.

COCKERELL, CHARLES ROBERT (1788–1863)
The son of S. P. Cockerell (q.v.), Charles made many visits to Greece and Rome before starting his architectural practice in 1817, aged twenty-nine. He subsequently used his immense archaeological erudition to great effect, being employed on a large number of public and domestic projects and designing numerous re-creations of ruined, antique sites. He also made an important contribution in emphasizing the ancient world's ubiquitous use of strong colour.

COCKERELL, SAMUEL PEPYS (1753–1827)
In Colvin's words, 'an able architect whose work is often interesting and original', he is best known for his 'Indian' fantasy houses in Gloucestershire: Daylesford (1788–93, for the notorious former Governor-General of India, Warren Hastings) and Sezincote (*c.*1805, for the architect's brother, Sir Charles Cockerell).

CRACE, JOHN (1754–1819)
The most renowned painter and decorator of the day, Crace's firm made its reputation with their astonishing work on the interiors at Brighton Pavilion after 1802, where both the Craces' skills (John was by now employing his son Frederick) at imitative painting, japanning, and gilding – still much in

evidence – were widely exploited. The firm was subsequently employed at other royal homes, notably the Prince's Carlton House. After 1817 Frederick took over the business, assisted by his brother Henry.

CUBITT, THOMAS (1788–1855)
The leading speculative builder-architect of the age, Cubitt (originally a ship's carpenter) developed large areas of Bloomsbury and Islington in the 1820s and subsequently created the vast, stuccoed seas of Pimlico and Belgravia to the south-west of Buckingham Palace.

FOULSTON, JOHN (1772–1842)
A keen Greek revivalist who idolized both Soane and Hope, his principal architectural achievements were in the city of Plymouth, where he lived most of his adult life. His ambitious plans to redevelop much of the city in the manner of Nash's stuccoed London terraces came to nothing, but he did win the commission for Plymouth's new Royal Hotel, Assembly Rooms, and Theatre (1811–13; demolished 1939–41). He is now principally known for his eccentric but powerful Egyptian façades.

GILLOW, ROBERT (c.1745–95) and RICHARD (1734–1811)
In 1729 Robert Gillow senior had founded the family furniture-making firm at Lancaster; on his death in 1772 the concern was taken over by his sons, Robert in London and Richard in Lancaster. The Gillows specialized in innovative furniture and invented such pieces as the telescopic dining table and the what-not. Much of their furniture can be identified by the special stamp they began using in the 1780s, although they also began to employ specific brand names for certain pieces, derived from the names of their aristocratic patrons. The firm also branched out into upholstery services and architectural joinery, such as chimneypieces and balusters; by 1800 whole houses were regularly being fitted and furnished entirely by the Gillows.

HOLLAND, HENRY (1745–1806)
One of the leading architects of the Late Georgian period, Holland was primarily responsible for introducing French and Neo-Classical influences into the mainstream of British architecture, producing a synthesis of these influences which was more chaste and refined than the style of the Adam brothers, so prevalent in the 1770s and 1780s. His reputation was secured by the commission to rebuild Carlton House in London for the Prince of Wales, a project which lasted from 1783 to 1796. Other influential commissions were the design for Sheridan's Drury Lane Theatre (built 1791–4) and the remodelling of Southill Park, Bedfordshire (1796–1800).

HOPE, THOMAS (1769–1831)
The son of a rich Amsterdam merchant, Hope came to England in 1795 and quickly established himself as a leading connoisseur and patron. Although only an amateur architect and designer, his publications – especially his *Household Furniture and Interior Decoration* of 1807 – exercised a great influence over contemporary taste. While his austere, Egyptian interiors were too extreme in their archaeological correctness

and bright colouration for most designers of the period, the radical style of his own homes at Duchess Street in London and Deepdene in Surrey helped to foster and popularize the Neo-Classical ideal.

JAY, WILLIAM (c. 1792–1837)
A native of Bath, Jay arrived in America in 1817 following an apprenticeship in the office of David Riddall Roper, a London architect and surveyor who had played a role in the rebuilding of Regent Street. Jay settled in Savannah, Georgia, where he enjoyed a wealthy and cultured clientele and little professional competition. His first work, a mansion completed in 1819 for Richard Richardson, is perhaps America's finest example of Regency domestic design. Other mansions followed, along with a theatre and a bank, all of them demonstrating a flair that marked Jay as one of the most talented architects practising in America at the time. In 1822, however, he returned to England, perhaps embittered by his faiure to obtain more widespread recognition. He designed a few more buildings in England, but at the time of his death was working as civil architect on the remote island of Mauritius.

LANNUIER, CHARLES-HONORE (1779–1819)
Lannuier emigrated to America from his native France in 1803 and advertised himself in the *New York Evening Post* as a maker of 'all kinds of furniture . . . in the newest and latest French Fashion'. He quickly established himself as the chief rival of Duncan Phyfe in the creation of fine furniture based on Regency and Empire developments in Europe. Lannuier's work is characterized by the use of rich materials and the excellence of detailing in such features as carved lion's-paw feet and ormolu mounts.

LATROBE, BENJAMIN (1764–1820)
Born in a Moravian community near Leeds, England, Latrobe became a pupil of the architect S. P. Cockerell (q.v.) in 1789. Soon after starting his own architectural practice, Latrobe found himself facing bankruptcy and decided to seek his fortune in America. In 1798 he won the commission to design the Bank of Philadelphia, a building that has been called 'the first monument of the Greek Revival in America'. From 1803 to 1817 he served as Surveyor of the US Capitol, in which capacity he made significant changes in the plans originally produced for the Capitol by William Thornton. During his tenure in Washington, Latrobe also designed St John's Church and Decatur House, both located on Lafayette Square facing the White House. His greatest monument, however, may be the Neo-Classical Roman Catholic cathedral he designed in Baltimore.

LOUDON, JOHN CLAUDIUS (1783–1843)
The son of a Scottish farmer, he came to London in 1803, and rapidly became a major – if not the principal – influence on Regency gardening and agriculture. His first book on gardening appeared in 1804; in 1809 he rented a farm near the idyllic Oxfordshire village of Great Tew and took pupils in agriculture. His *Encyclopaedia of Agriculture* of 1825 and *Encyclopaedia of Plants* of 1829 were followed by the hugely popular *Encyclopaedia of Cottage, Farm and Villa Architecture and Furniture* of 1833 – a complete guide to the disposition,

furnishing, and decoration of the average house and garden. In 1838 this concept was extended by *The Suburban Gardener and Villa Companion* and the financially disastrous *Arboretum*, an encyclopaedia of British trees and shrubs. Although disabled (he lost his right arm in 1825) and constantly ill, he remained active as a writer until his death.

MILLS, ROBERT (1781–1855)

Mills has a good claim to the title of America's first native-born professionally trained architect. Born in South Carolina, Mills travelled to Washington, DC, at the age of nineteen. Thomas Jefferson introduced him to Benjamin Latrobe (q.v.), with whom Mills worked for several years. By 1812, Mills had launched his own successful practice; in fact, his design that year for the Monumental Church in Richmond was chosen over one submitted by Latrobe. His bright prospects blighted by an economic depression, he accepted a position directing public improvements in South Carolina, where he designed dozens of canals, courthouses, jails and other public buildings across the state. Returning to Washington in 1830, Mills was eventually responsible for the design of some of the capital's most important public buildings, including the US Treasury Building, the Patent Office (now the National Portrait Gallery) and the General Post Office. He also designed two famous monuments to George Washington: a colossal column in Baltimore which was the first major memorial to the Father of His Country, and the world-famous 555-foot-high obelisk which still dominates the Washington skyline.

NASH, JOHN (1752–1835)

Prior to forming a partnership with the renowned landscape gardener Humphry Repton (q.v.), Nash was principally known during the 1790s and early 1800s as a designer of picturesque villas. After 1811, however, he found greater fame as the Prince Regent's principal architect, in which capacity he laid out the new gardens and streets of London's Crown-owned Regent's Park development during the 1820s and drastically remodelled Brighton Pavilion in a 'Chinese' style in 1815–21. His work for George IV at Buckingham Palace was, like all his projects, enormously expensive, and he was heavily criticized in Parliament and in the press. His intimate links with George IV (he would have been created a baronet by the latter but for Wellington's stubborn opposition) meant that his career was effectively terminated by the King's death in 1830. By the time of his own death, five years later, his buildings were being commonly reviled by the new generation of architects.

PAPWORTH, JOHN BUONARROTI (1775–1847)

Trained as a sculptor, decorator, and painter, Papworth was a prolific architect whose books – particularly *Rural Residences* of 1818 – were hugely influential on contemporaries. His wide-ranging talents encompassed gardening (cf. his *Hints on Ornamental Gardening* of 1823), silver design, monumental statuary, town planning, and work in glass (which included a glass throne for the Shah of Persia). He contributed many designs to Ackermann's *Repository* and designed Ackermann's own offices of 1826. His son later alleged that many of the designs of Loudon's *Encyclopaedia* of 1833 were in fact stolen from his father.

PHYFE, DUNCAN (1768–1854)

Probably the best-known of all American cabinet-makers, Phyfe was first listed as a practitioner of the trade in the *New York Directory and Register* in 1794, approximately ten years after emigrating from Scotland. Within another ten years, his workshops, showrooms and warehouse had expanded to fill three buildings, and he eventually employed about one hundred men. His designs were not innovative, never straying far from English prototypes or the work of his New York contemporaries, and his products were intended for a wide public. At its best, however, Phyfe's furniture bears comparison with the finest work of Regency England, and his name has become synonymous with high-quality design and craftsmanship.

PUGIN, AUGUSTUS CHARLES (1769–1832)

Arriving in Britain as a refugee from revolutionary France, with little English and a dubious aristocratic background, Pugin was taken up by John Nash as a draughtsman. By 1799, when he exhibited at the Royal Academy, he was the most celebrated draughtsman of his day. His plates and drawings of authentic medieval architecture did much to popularize the late Regency fashion for the Gothic style; indeed, his Gothic plates for Ackermann's *Repository* (published in 1825–7, reprinted together as *Gothic Furniture* in 1827) can be said to have kindled the popular enthusiasm for Gothic.

PUGIN, AUGUSTUS WELBY NORTHMORE (1812–52)

The son of A. C. Pugin (q.v.), in 1827 – when only twelve years old – he was commissioned to design items of Gothic furniture for Windsor Castle, in the vein of his father's pieces. He subsequently established his own cabinet-making firm, and while he later became the leading spirit of the Early Victorian Gothic Revival, during the 1830s he was primarily known as a furniture designer and as a vociferous critic of the forms and techniques of Regency Classicism, his vehemence on the latter subject being expressed with great clarity and force in his prophetic and virulent book *Contrasts* of 1836.

REPTON, HUMPHRY (1752–1818)

Having begun a career as a merchant, Repton then studied gardening and was soon established as a leading landscape gardener – famous for his theories of the picturesque and for the lavishly illustrated 'Red Book' reports with which he presented his clients. Although not trained as an architect, he designed a number of small cottages and garden temples. By the time of his death he was sufficiently famous to be immortalized by Jane Austen and for his work to be satirized by Thomas Love Peacock; his observations on landscape gardening and garden architecture, however, were not to reach a wide audience until the publication of Loudon's *The Landscape Gardening and Landscape Architecture of the late Humphry Repton* in 1840.

SHERATON, THOMAS (1751–1806)

The son of a 'mechanic' of Stockton-on-Tees, he trained in the cabinet-making trade and, already a keen and pious Baptist who had published several religious tracts, came to London in 1790. His *Cabinet-Maker and Upholsterer's Drawing Book*, published in fortnightly instalments between 1791 and 1793, was one of the most influential pattern-books of the Regency period, introducing America, France, and Germany, as well as Britain, to an advanced Regency style. The *Cabinet Dictionary* of 1803 was similarly seminal; however, his last book, *The Cabinet-Maker, Upholsterer, and General Artist's Encyclopaedia*, was, in the words of Beard and Gilbert, 'a discursive rambling work displaying symptoms of the mental debility that preceded his death'. Only thirty of the 125 parts had actually appeared before Sheraton died, penniless and insane, in 1806.

SMITH, GEORGE (c.1786–1826)

Trained as a cabinet-maker, Smith – having survived two bankruptcies in 1790 – made his name as a talented yet pragmatic furniture designer, with the publication in 1808 of his *A Collection of Designs for Household Furniture and Interior Decoration*, a work which capitalized on the novelty (and title) of Hope's book of the preceding year, and in which he rather audaciously described himself as 'upholder [upholsterer] extraordinary to his Royal Highness the Prince of Wales'. He tamed and popularized the severe Neo-Classicism of Hope (q.v.) and Tatham (q.v.) but could also turn his hand to Chinese, Gothic, or Louis XVI styles. His later books were equally popular: *A Collection of Ornamental Designs* of 1812, and *The Cabinet-Maker and Upholsterer's Guide*, in which he now claimed the post of 'Upholsterer and Furniture Draughtsman to His Majesty'.

SOANE, SIR JOHN (1753–1837)

As an architectural student, Soane served as Holland's assistant and by 1790 had built up a sizeable architectural practice of his own. A difficult man, he was nevertheless a designer of vast originality, responsible for the new Bank of England (1788–1833) and a large number of country and town houses. His mannered, eclectic style and rich, antique colours can still be seen in his own home at 12–13 Lincoln's Inn Fields, London (now housing Sir John Soane's Museum), the restored interiors of Pitshanger Manor (1800–3) in Ealing, west London, and Dulwich College Picture Gallery (1811–14) in south London. Knighted in 1832, in 1834 he was offered the first Presidency of the new Institute of British Architects – which, as a Royal Academician, he had to refuse.

TATHAM, CHARLES HEATHCOTE (1772–1842)

Like Sheraton a native of Stockton-on-Tees. Tatham's severe and idealized Neo-Classical designs did not win him many eager patrons. However, his books – principally his *Etchings* of 1799–1800, culled from his drawings executed while Holland's agent in Rome in 1794–7 – proved a source-book of great influence on designers such as Hope (q.v.) and George Smith (q.v.). His designs were not limited to architecture and furniture; witness his *Designs for Ornamental Plate* of 1806.

WILDS, AMON (c.1762–1833)

In the early 1820 Wilds – originally an architect in Lewes, Sussex, but since 1815 living with his son and partner in Brighton – went into partnership with the local architect Charles Busby (q.v.), with whom he transformed vast areas of Brighton from fields and wasteland into the vast stuccoed squares and terraces which so distinguish modern Brighton. His son, Amon Henry Wilds (d. c.1849), also practised as an architect in the town, building himself a riotously Gothick home on Western Road (still extant, but much mutilated), the Regency Gothic Silwood Place of 1827, and inventing a new classical order based on the ammonite – a grating pun on his own name.

WYATT, JAMES (1746–1813)

A hugely prolific architect who embraced a wide variety of styles – from the antique Roman of the Oxford Street Pantheon (1770–2) via the Greek Revival of his country houses to the celebrated Gothic piles of Ashridge, Hertfordshire (1808–13) and the ill-fated 'abbey' of Fonthill, Wiltshire (1796–1812). Wyatt has been much criticized, both by contemporaries and by a torrent of more modern critics, for his unscholarly, careless, and even unprincipled attitude to construction and repair. While Fonthill represents the apogee of the romantic Regency Gothic, his numerous, heavy-handed cathedral restorations have been repeatedly denounced over the past two centuries. His son, Benjamin Dean Wyatt (d. c.1855), also became a noted architect.

WYATT, SAMUEL (1737–1807)

Elder brother of James (q.v.), he trained under Robert Adam, and later specialized in severely Neo-Classical country houses – most notably the remodelled Shugborough, Staffordshire (for the legendary Admiral Anson, 1790–8) – and in designing cottages, lodges, barns, and model farms in an appropriately antique vein.

WYATVILLE, SIR JEFFRY (1766–1840)

Born plain Jeffry Wyatt, in 1824 this very average architect secured royal patronage as the architect hired to transform Windsor Castle to an aspect which accorded more with George IV's grandiosely romantic – and vastly expensive – tastes. The King immediately gave Wyatt leave to make his name more pretentiously francophone and in 1828 knighted him. In contrast to the treatment meted out to George IV's other architectural protégé, Nash (q.v.), Wyatville's designs survived a House of Commons inquiry, and while his Royal Lodge in Windsor Great Park was immediately demolished on George's death, work on Windsor Castle continued throughout the 1830s.

Acanthus
Plant with thick leaves which is used as a decorative motif on antique Corinthian and Composite (a hybrid mixture of Ionic and Corinthian) CAPITALS, and which in Regency Britain was much used on all types of classical MOULDINGS.

Acroterion
Originally a plinth to carry an ornament placed at the summit or the corner of a PEDIMENT. In the Regency period, acroteria were more usually quadrant-shaped 'ears' at the corners of pediments or cabinet tops.

Anthemion
Ornamental motif based on the honeysuckle flower and leaves; much used in the Regency period for MOULDINGS and ironwork.

Architrave
Moulded door or window surround. In strict classical terms, the lowest part of the ENTABLATURE (above the CAPITAL and below the FRIEZE).

Ashlar
Smoothly dressed, coursed stonework, with very narrow joints.

Astragal
Small, semicircular-profiled MOULDING; also section of window glazing bar.

Baize
Heavy woollen cloth, well felted, and often dyed green or brown.

Bead
Small MOULDING dating from the Norman era, with a semicircular profile; continuous, or resembling a string of beads. Often recessed (e.g. when separating elements of the door) and flush with adjacent surfaces.

Bombazine
Heavy fabric of silk warp and WORSTED weft, usually made in Norwich. Generally used for dressmaking, but also as a heavy-duty furnishing fabric.

Boulle (or **Bühl**)
Decorative work formed by glueing together sheets of brass and tortoiseshell (or other like materials), the upper sheet being subsequently engraved in a pattern.

Buckram
A coarse hemp cloth, used to stiffen upholstery or valances, being inserted behind the surface material.

Calico
Strong cotton cloth, resembling linen; its name comes from one of its original sources – 'Calicut', in Portuguese India. Made in Britain from the 1770s.

Cambric
Fine white linen cloth.

Canvas
Very coarse hemp or flax (linen) cloth; also known as bolting.

Capital
Head of a column or PILASTER; often decorated, according to the type of ORDER used. Regency architects such as Soane and Wilds frequently departed from the five antique ORDERS to invent their own, with fantastical capitals based on native plants and animals.

Caryatid
Column or PILASTER in the shape of a female figure. The male equivalents (which usually wore a more solemn if not tragic expression) were called atlantes or telamones.

Casement
Traditional medieval window type; side- or top-hung, and opening inwards or outwards. Largely replaced by the sash window throughout the Georgian period.

Cassimere
Medium-weight, soft, twilled woollen cloth; a cheaper version of cashmere.

Chiffonier
Commode or sideboard with open shelves (although some were provided with doors).

Chimera
Fabulous animal, much used by Hope and subsequent practitioners of the Egyptian style, with the wings of an eagle, the head and body of a lion, and the tail of a dragon.

Chintz
Printed or possibly even painted cotton, sometimes glazed to be more washable and hard-wearing. Originally from India, where 'chitta' meant 'spotted cloth'.

Coade stone
Durable ceramic, made in Lambeth by Eleanor Coade after 1769, which could mimic stone or plaster (see Chapter Three).

Corduroy
Durable cotton, with the weft raised in ribs.

Cornice
The upper part of the ENTABLATURE, or the uppermost part of a wall. Also applies to any projecting MOULDING at the top of internal or external walls.

Damask
Reversible patterned fabric, usually in one single colour; the pattern is produced by the contrast between the warp and weft faces, the former producing the satin ground.

Deal
Planks of fir or pine; from the Low German *dele*, meaning plank. Generally imported from the Baltic or from North America.

Dentil
Plain projecting MOULDING with a square profile. Repeated dentils often featured in simple CORNICES.

Dimity
Any type of plain or patterned fabric. White dimity was often used as a furnishing fabric in humbler houses and cottages – particularly in the countryside, where it was not affected by industrial dirt.

Drugget
Thin cloth, often used to cover floors or carpets, or as a loose cover for furniture; half wool and half linen, usually twilled.

Entablature
Upper part of the classical ORDERS, above the CAPITAL; consists of ARCHITRAVE, FRIEZE, and CORNICE.

Frieze
Middle section of the ENTABLATURE, below the CORNICE. Often decorated with motifs or representational carvings. Also used for the equivalent section of a wall, i.e. the wide band below the CORNICE of a room.

Gadrooning
Repeated pattern of a flowing and convex nature.

Gauffering
Process by which areas of pile fabrics were pressed to make a pattern. After *c.*1830 this was largely accomplished mechanically.

Gauze
Thin, transparent fabric with a crossed-warp weave.

Gimp
A decorative, openwork band of stiff thread, often used as a border or edging for furnishing fabrics.

Gingham
Striped or checked cotton. Often used in the Regency period for cheap bedroom hangings or loose furniture covers.

Guilloche
Decorative MOULDING comprising interlaced S's; much used during the Regency, especially on the soffits of structural members.

Japanning
Term originally used for coloured lacquering (usually black or red) on imported Japanese cabinets. Oriental lacquer was derived from plants, whereas English black lacquer was manufactured synthetically from asphaltum or candle soot. By the Regency the term was used for any effect obtained by built-up layers of lacquering – whether on wood, papier mâché, or metals.

Linsey-woolsey
A coarse and cheap furnishing fabric, with a linen warp and woollen weft.

Lustrene
Woollen cloth, pressed hard to give a smooth finish.

Manchester velvet
Cotton velvet produced in Manchester. Hugely popular as a cheap but impressive furnishing fabric in the Regency period.

Mastic
Oil-based render or plaster.

Mathematical tile
Clay tile with a large nib, laid on a vertical wall in interlocking courses to give the appearance of brickwork. Much used during the Regency period, the centre for the production of these tiles was Kent and Sussex.

Merino
Soft woollen cloth from the wool of the merino sheep, which was first introduced to England by George III. In 1809 the *Repository* lauded the old King's 'unwearied and patriotic effort for [the sheep's] increase and diffusion'.

Modillion
Scroll-shaped bracket appearing in the CORNICE or supporting a structural or projecting member.

Moire
Ribbed or grained silk.

Monopodium
Furniture support in the shape of a sphinx or animal head, incorporated into a single leg and foot.

Moreen
WORSTED cloth with a waved or stamped finish. This 'watered' look was very fashionable during the early Regency but soon fell out of favour as more easily washable fabrics became available.

Moulding
Contour or pattern given to projecting surfaces in architecture or furniture; generally executed in plaster, papier mâché, or wood.

Muslin
Fine cotton textile originating in India. Used to make transparent sub-curtains which would filter the direct light entering a room.

Order
Classical architectural formula of column and ENTABLATURE which formed the basis for all Greek and Roman architecture. The five Graeco-Roman orders comprised the Doric (the plainest), Tuscan, Ionic, Corinthian, and Composite (the most elaborately decorated).

Ormolu
Gilded alloy of copper, zinc, and tin; much used for mounts, frames, and furniture decoration. 'English ormolu' referred to the simple lacquering of brass or similar alloy to get the same lustrous effect.

Palmette
Fan-shaped leaf ornament resembling a palm leaf; often used in conjunction with the ANTHEMION.

Patera
Flat circular or oval ornament, often decorated with a flower pattern. Much used in Regency architecture, particularly at the corners of panels and surrounds.

Pediment
Classical architectural termination, either triangular or segmental (i.e. with a curved upper surface).

Pilaster
Flat-faced column projecting from a masonry or panelled surface. Not to be confused with an engaged column, which refers to the effect by which a normal, cylindrical column appears to have half of (or part of) its shaft buried in the wall behind.

Quirk
Sharp incision or undercutting between MOULDINGS or adjacent surfaces, designed to throw more shadows. Very commonly used during the Regency.

Quoin
Stone or brick at the right-angled corner of a building; generally projecting from the wall surface to emphasize the termination.

Rail
Horizontal member of a door or window, or of a piece of furniture. The meeting rails of a sash window are those two rails which interlock when the sash is shut and which carry the sash fasteners.

Reeding
Characteristic Regency MOULDING formed from combined BEADS or similar groups of other simple convex mouldings.

Render
Plaster covering of a wall. A general term which includes stucco and even interior (gypsum) plaster; now used generally to indicate an exterior covering.

Serge
A twilled fabric with a WORSTED warp and woollen weft.

Settee
Multi-seated chair. Distinct from a sofa in being derived directly from the form, height, and pattern of adjacent chairs.

Stile
Vertical structural members of a door, window, or piece of furniture.

Stock
Originally, the board on which a brick was hand-shaped; by the late eighteenth century this term, short for 'stock brick', indicated an average-strength brick of reasonable quality and finish. 'London stocks', grey or yellow facing bricks (their colour deriving from the local clays), were much used in the speculative building of the period.

String course
Projecting masonry course (i.e. horizontal band) on the exterior of a wall.

Stuff
General term referring to WORSTED cloths.

Taffeta
Plain-woven silk, with thicker weft threads. Popular for window and bed hangings.

Term
A pedestal topped with a human or animal figure, tapering towards the bottom. Stone, plaster, or COADE terms were often used as garden ornaments.

Ticking
Linen twill, often striped.

Tuck pointing
The process by which inferior or badly-cut bricks are set in a mortar of the same colour as the brick itself; in order to give the impression of expensive, thin-jointed brickwork, a straight line of white 'tucking' mortar is then set into this original mortar.

Velveteen
A looped-pile fabric intended to be an inferior, cheaper substitute for cotton or silk velvet.

Verre églomisé
Engraved gold leaf under a protective surface of glass.

Vitruvian scroll
Wave ornament often used to decorate Regency friezes. Also called 'running dog'. The name is derived from the ancient Roman architect Marcus Vitruvius Pollio, whose works were an enormous influence on the Classical revival of Western Europe.

What-not
Small table with open shelves, possibly invented by Sheraton.

Worsted
Wool yarn which is combed before spinning to give a smoother effect.

If you are seeking to repair, renovate, or redecorate your Regency home, the following sources of information can help not only with methods of repair and types of materials but also with advice on suitable local suppliers and craftsmen.

Remember, many directories of suppliers and services which pose as authoritative and critical guides to the best experts in the subject are actually nothing of the sort. Neither are salesmen the best sources of balanced information about their own products. It is always important to get the advice of a disinterested expert before you begin any type of repair or redecoration.

CONTACTS AND SOURCES OF INFORMATION IN THE UNITED KINGDOM

1 CONSERVATION OFFICERS

The Conservation Officer of your local District or Borough Council (usually associated with the council's Planning Department) is there specifically to help house owners on all aspects of period house renovation. He or she can advise on local joiners, plasterers, ironworkers, and other good, reliable craftsmen in the area. They can also let you know about possible local authority grant aid for your repairs or alterations. Some county councils also have expert conservation groups who can be of similar help.

Architectural salvage outlets can be very useful. They can also be horribly misused, encouraging over-enthusiastic house owners to install over-sized or over-elaborate elements in inappropriate settings. Also, while some salvage companies are exemplary in their dealings with suppliers and public alike, others are not so scrupulous – at worst effectively acting as fences for the hugely expanding trade in art and architectural theft. As with local craftsmen, do not just rely on consulting the Yellow Pages or a magazine directory to get the names of random architectural salvage companies; talk to your local Conservation Officer before choosing one.

If your building is listed, your Conservation Officer should also be able to provide you with details of the listing, which should tell you more about the history of your home.

2 ENGLISH HERITAGE

As the principal body regulating the conservation and maintenance of historic buildings in England, English Heritage (officially known as the Historic Buildings and Monuments Commission), and its equivalents in Wales (Cadw) and Scotland (Heritage in Scotland), are well equipped to help in a variety of ways.

The Research and Technical Advice Service Conservation Section of English Heritage in London (Keysign House, 429 Oxford St, London W1R 2HD, tel. 071 973 3000) can advise on all matters of repair or redecoration. John and Nicola Ashurst produced a five-volume series on *Practical Building Conservation* for the section in 1988; this series, which is available from English Heritage or from good bookshops, is easily the best guide to problems and solutions in the area of repair and maintenance. The subjects covered include stone masonry (vol. 1); terracotta, brick, and earth (vol. 2); mortars,

plasters, and renders (vol. 3); metals (vol. 4); and wood, glass, and resins (vol. 5).

English Heritage's Architectural Study Collection, also run from Keysign House, is an excellent source of decorative treatments and artefacts, from Regency roller blinds to original wallpaper. The experts who administer the Collection also have a wide knowledge of structural and decorative solutions for all types of building. Contact them on 071 973 3637.

Locally, the local English Heritage historic buildings inspector should be able to help with methods of repair and types of decoration, as well as with reliable local suppliers. He or she may even be able to visit your home to give on-the-spot advice. To find out who your local inspector is, ring the general English Heritage number (071 973 3000).

3 NATIONAL AMENITY SOCIETIES

The National Amenity Societies not only serve as legal consultees on alterations to listed buildings involving demolition but also offer advisory services on all aspects of period homes, whether listed or not.

The Georgian Group (37 Spital Square, London E1 6DY, tel. 071 377 1722) produce a series of introductory guides on key aspects of the Georgian house. The series currently comprises: No. 1 *Windows*, No. 2 *Brickwork*, No. 3 *Doors*, No. 4 *Paint Colour*, No. 5 *Render, Plaster and Stucco*, No. 6 *Wallpaper*, No. 7 *Mouldings*, No. 8 *Ironwork*, No. 9 *Fireplaces*, No. 10 *Roofs*, No. 11 *Floors*, No. 12 *Stonework*, No. 13 *Lighting*, and No. 14 Curtains and Blinds. Nos. 4 and 6 include lists of UK manufacturers and suppliers of traditional paints and of reproductions of Georgian wallpapers respectively. The Group also produces general booklists for those beginning or contemplating repair or redecoration.

The Society for the Protection of Ancient Buildings (37 Spital Square, London E1 6DY, tel. 071 377 1644) publishes a large series of cheap but invaluable Technical Pamphlets and more basic Information Sheets on most aspects of maintenance and repair. They can also advise on suitable surveyors and good joiners, plasterers, and craftsmen in related fields. The Society additionally produces a quarterly *Period Property Register* of historic houses for sale.

4 SPECIALIST SOCIETIES AND PROFESSIONAL ORGANIZATIONS

The Garden History Society
5 The Knoll
Hereford HR1 1RU

The Furniture History Society
Flat 1
78 Redcliffe Square
London SW10 9BN

The Wallpaper History Society
c/o Furniture and Interiors Department
The Victoria and Albert Museum
South Kensington
London SW7 2RL

The Tiles & Architectural Ceramics Society
Reabrook Lodge
8 Sutton Road
Shrewsbury
Shropshire SY2 6DD

The British Brick Society
Woodside House
Winkfield
Windsor
Berks SL4 2DX

The Brick Advisory Centre
The Building Centre
26 Store Street
London WC1E 7BT

The Glass and Glazing Federation
44 Borough High Street
London SE1 1XB

5 MUSEUMS

Local and national museums often serve as sources of
expert knowledge on internal and external decoration.
Prominent among these are:

The Department of Furniture and Interiors
The Victoria and Albert Museum
South Kensington
London SW7 2RL

Temple Newsam House
Temple Newsam Park
Leeds LS15 0AE

Heaton Hall
Heaton
Manchester M25 5SW

Aston Hall
Trinity Road
Aston
Birmingham B6 7JD

Conservation Department
Brighton Pavilion
The Steine
Brighton BN1 1UE

The Brooking Collection
Thames Polytechnic
Brewhouse Lane
Wapping
London E1 9NU
(A vast collection of architectural artefacts, including
doors, windows, glazing bars, sash mechanisms, fanlights, and
ironwork. View by appointment.)

York Castle Museum
York YO1 1RY
(Includes a collection of kitchen equipment.)

Museum of English Rural Life
Reading University
Whiteknights
PO Box 229
Reading RG6 2AG
(A large collection of kitchen and other servicing equipment.)

6 HOUSES OPEN TO THE PUBLIC

Included below is a list of British Regency houses
open to the public which have interiors in a
reasonably original state. While these may be very
useful sources of reference, remember that the scale,
complexity, and pretension of their interiors may be
inappropriate for the more modest dimensions and
differing character of your own home.

Pitshanger Manor Museum
Mattock Lane
Ealing
London W5 5EQ

Sir John Soane's Museum
13 Lincoln's Inn Fields
London WC2A 3BP

Apsley House
Hyde Park Corner
London W1V 9FA

Keats House
Wentworth Place
Keats Grove
London NW3 2RR

Brighton Pavilion
The Steine
Brighton BN1 1UE

Shugborough
Milford
Staffordshire ST17 0XB
(National Trust)

Attingham Park
Shrewsbury
Shropshire SY4 4TP
(National Trust)

CONTACTS AND SOURCES OF INFORMATION
IN THE UNITED STATES

1 STATE HISTORIC PRESERVATION OFFICES

Each state has a designated State Historic Preservation Officer (SHPO) whose responsibilities include carrying out statewide inventories of cultural resources, nominating properties to the National Register of Historic Places, operating grant and loan programmes, administering historic properties, and providing public education and information. Your SHPO can be an invaluable source of guidance and advice on proper preservation techniques, on the National Register nomination procedure, on the requirements for federal tax credits for rehabilitation, and on a number of other subjects. A list of SHPOs can be found in *Landmark Yellow Pages* (see 'Further Reading' section).

2 STATEWIDE AND LOCAL PRESERVATION ORGANIZATIONS

Local preservation organizations exist in hundreds of communities, bringing together preservationists for educational programmes, conducting tours of historic homes and neighbourhoods, offering advice on preservation techniques and sources of assistance, and issuing newsletters and other publications. In addition, statewide preservation groups exist in many states, linking local groups with one another, lobbying for state and local legislation supportive of preservation interests, administering funding programmes, and serving as information clearing-houses. Your National Trust regional office (see below) may be able to provide the names of statewide and local organizations in your area.

3 LOCAL HISTORIC DISTRICT COMMISSIONS

If your house has been designated a local landmark or is situated in a locally designated historic district, you may be required to obtain the approval of a review board before making certain alterations to the property. Titles of these boards vary widely – 'historic district commission', 'design review board', 'board of architectural review', and so on – as do the provisions of the ordinances which they administer. Check with the city hall (the planning and zoning commission is a good place to start) for information on whether your house or neighbourhood is governed by local preservation regulations.

4 HISTORIC AMERICAN BUILDINGS SURVEY

Founded in the 1930s, the Historic American Buildings Survey (HABS) is an invaluable collection of photographs, measured drawings and documentary research on hundreds of historic structures. To find out whether a particular property may have been documented by HABS, or to obtain copies of photos and drawings of documented structures, contact:

Historic American Buildings Survey
Division of Prints and Photographs
Library of Congress
Washington, DC 20540
202 707-6394

5 NATIONAL TRUST FOR HISTORIC PRESERVATION

Chartered by Congress in 1949, the National Trust is a nationwide nonprofit organization with more than 250,000 members. The Trust publishes a monthly newspaper, *Historic Preservation News*, a bimonthly magazine, *Historic Preservation*, and a wide variety of books and other materials; conducts conferences, workshops and seminars on a range of preservation-related topics; supports the work of local and statewide preservation organizations; administers a nationwide collection of historic museum properties; and, through its network of regional offices, offers advice and information to preservationists. For general membership information, contact:

National Trust for Historic Preservation
1785 Massachusetts Avenue, NW
Washington, DC 20036
202 673-4000

For information on a particular subject, contact the appropriate regional office:

Mid-Atlantic Regional Office
6401 Germantown Avenue
Philadelphia, PA 19144
215 438-2886
(DE, DC, MD, NJ, PA, VA, WV, Puerto Rico, Virgin Islands)

Midwest Regional Office
53 West Jackson Boulevard, Suite 1135
Chicago, IL 60604
312 939-5547
(IL, IN, IA, MI, MN, MO, OH, WI)

Northeast Regional Office
7 Faneuil Hall Marketplace, 5th Floor
Boston, MA 02109
617 523-0885
(CT, ME, MA, NH, NY, RI, VT)

Southern Regional Office
456 King Street
Charleston, SC 29403
803 722-8552
(AL, AR, FL, GA, KY, LA, MS, NC, SC, TN)

Mountains/Plains Regional Office
511 16th Street, Suite 700
Denver, CO 80202
303 623-1504
(CO, KS, MT, NE, ND, OK, SD, WY)

Texas/New Mexico Field Office
500 Main Street, Suite 606
Fort Worth, TX 76102
817 332-4398
(NM, TX)

Western Regional Office
One Sutter Street, Suite 707
San Francisco, CA 94104
415 956-0610
(AK, AZ, CA, HI, ID, NV, OR, UT, WA, Guam, Micronesia)

6 OLD-HOUSE JOURNAL

Published bimonthly, the *Old-House Journal* is an excellent source of 'how-to' advice for the handyman, as well as information of interest to the old-house *aficionado*. In addition to the magazine itself, the *Journal* also publishes an annual catalogue that lists sources of traditional products for the old home. For subscription information, contact:

Old-House Journal
PO Box 50214
Boulder, CO 80321
(800) 888-9070

7 OTHER ORGANIZATIONS

American Association for State and Local History
172 2nd Avenue, North
Suite 202
Nashville, TN 37201

Decorative Arts Society
c/o Brooklyn Museum
200 Eastern Parkway
Brooklyn, NY 11238

Society of Architectural Historians
1232 Pine Street
Philadelphia, PA 19107

8 MUSEUMS

Cooper-Hewitt National Museum of Design
2 East 91st Street
New York, NY 10128

Diplomatic Reception Rooms
US Department of State
2201 C Street, NW
Washington, DC 20520

Henry Francis du Pont Winterthur Museum
Route 52
Winterthur, DE 19735

Metropolitan Museum of Art
5th Avenue at 82nd Street
New York, NY 10028

Museum of Fine Arts
465 Huntington Avenue
Boston, MA 02115

Philadelphia Museum of Art
26th Street and Benjamin Franklin Parkway
Philadelphia, PA 19130

9 HOUSES OPEN TO THE PUBLIC

Aiken-Rhett House
48 Elizabeth Street
Charleston, SC

Edmonston-Alston House
21 East Battery
Charleston, SC

Hyde Hall
Glimmerglass State Park
East Springfield, NY

Richardson-Owens-Thomas House
124 Abercorn Street
Savannah, GA

William Scarbrough House
41 West Broad Street
Savannah, GA

Place of publication London unless otherwise stated

Introduction
THE REGENCY

(a) Contemporary sources

Austen, Jane, *Mansfield Park*, 1814
——, *Northanger Abbey*, 1818
Dickens, Charles, *The Pickwick Papers*, 1836–7
Moses, H., *Modern Costumes*, 1812
Pyne, W. H., *A History of the Royal Residences*, 1819
Southey, Robert ('Don Manuel Espriella'), *Letters from England*, 1807

(b) Modern sources

Carlton House: The Past Glories of George IV's Palace (The Queen's Gallery, Buckingham Palace, exh. cat.)
Cornforth, John, *English Interiors 1790–1848*, 1978
Cruickshank, Dan, and Neil Burton, *Life in the Georgian City*, 1990
George, M. Dorothy, *London Life in the 18th Century*, 1965
Hibbert, Christopher, *George IV*, 1976
Musgrave, Clifford, *Life in Brighton*, 1970
Porter, Roy, *Life in Eighteenth Century England*, 1977
Rudé, George, *Hanoverian London*, 19xx
Ziegler, Philip, *William IV*, 1971

Chapter One
THE ARCHITECTURAL SHELL

(a) Architects

Colvin, Howard, *A Biographical Dictionary of British Architects 1600–1840*, 1978
Hamlin, Talbot, *Benjamin Henry Latrobe*, New York, 1955
Hobhouse, Hermione, *Thomas Cubitt, Master Builder*, 1971
Hussey, Christopher, *English Country Houses: Late Georgian*, 1955
Mowl, Tim, 'The Williamane: Architecture for the Sailor King' in R. White and C. Lightburn, eds., *Late Georgian Classicism*, 1989
Robinson, John Martin, *The Wyatts: An Architectural Dynasty*, 1979
Stroud, Dorothy, *The Architecture of Sir John Soane*, 1961
——, *Henry Holland, His Life and Architecture*, 1966
Summerson, John, *The Life and Work of John Nash*, 1980
——, *Georgian London*, 1989
Watkin, David, *Thomas Hope and the Neo-Classical Idea*, 1968
——, *The Life and Work of C. R. Cockerell*, 1974
Worsley, Giles, *Architectural Drawings of the Regency Period*, 1991

(b) Construction

Amery, Colin, *Three Centuries of Architectural Craftsmanship*, 1978
——, *Period Houses and their Details*, 1978

Ashurst, John and Nicola, *Practical Building Conservation*, vols. 1–5 (Stone Masonry; Terracotta, Brick and Earth; Mortars, Plasters and Renders; Metals; Wood, Glass and Resins), 1988
Clifton-Taylor, Alec, and R. W. Brunskill, *English Brickwork*, 1977
Cox, Alan, *Brickmaking*, Bedfordshire County Council, 1979
Cruickshank, Dan, and Peter Wyld, *London: The Art of Georgian Building*, 1975
Hayward, Robert, *The Brick Book*, 1978
Kelly, Alison, *Mrs Coade's Stone*, 1990
Kelsall, Frank, 'Stucco' in Hermione Hobhouse and Ann Sanders, eds., *Good and Proper Materials*, London Topographical Society, 1989
Lloyd, Nathaniel, *A History of English Brickwork*, 1925; 1983
Saunders, Matthew, *The Historic Home Owner's Companion*, 1987

Chapter Two
DOORS AND WINDOWS

Davie, W. G., and G. Tanner, *Old English Doors*, 1903
Douglas, R. W., and S. Frank, *A History of Glassmaking*, 1972
Parissien, Steven, *Doors* and *Windows* (The Georgian Group Guides), 1989
Sambrook, John, *Fanlights*, 1989

Chapter Three
JOINERY AND PLASTERWORK

Chatwin, Anna, *Cheltenham's Ornamental Ironwork*, Cheltenham, 1974
Diestelkamp, Edward, 'Building Technology and Architecture 1790–1830' in R. White and C. Lightburn, eds., *Late Georgian Classicism*, 1989
Gilbert, C., J. Lomax, and A. Wells-Cole, *Country House Floors*, Leeds City Art Galleries, 1987
Nicholson, Peter, *Mechanical Exercises*, 1812
——, *The New and Improved Practical Builder*, 1823

Chapter Four
SERVICES

Brears, Peter, *The Kitchen Catalogue*, York Castle Museum, 1979
Eveleigh, David, *Firegrates and Kitchen Ranges*, 1983
Field, Rachel, *Irons in the Fire: A History of Cooking Equipment*, 1984
Gilbert, C., and A. Wells-Cole, *The Fashionable Fire-Place*, Leeds City Art Galleries, 1985
Moncrieff, Elspeth, 'Argand Lamps', *The Antique Collector*, February 1990, pp. 46–53

Chapter Five
COLOURS AND COVERINGS

(a) Contemporary sources

'A Lady', *The Workwoman's Guide*, 1838
Butcher, William, *Smith's Art of House Painting*, 1821
Hay, D. R., *The Laws of Harmonious Colouring*, 1821
Loudon, J. C., *An Encyclopaedia of Cottage, Farm and Villa Architecture*, 1833
Whittock, Nathaniel, *The Decorative Painter's and Glazier's Guide*, 1827

(b) Modern sources

Agius, Pauline, ed., *Ackermann's Regency Furniture and Interiors*, 1984
Collard, Frances, *Regency Furniture*, 1985
Entwisle, E. A., *The Book of Wallpaper*, 1970
Gere, Charlotte, *Nineteenth-Century Decoration*, 1989
Greysmith, Brenda, *Wallpaper*, 1976
Jameson, Clare, ed., *A Pictorial Treasury of Curtain and Drapery Designs 1750–1950*, 1987
Lynn, Catherine, *Wallpapers in America*, 1980
Montgomery, Florence, *Printed Textiles: English and American Cottons and Linens 1700–1850*, 1970
——, *Textiles in America*, New York, 1984
Oman, Charles, and Jean Hamilton, *Wallpapers*, 1982
Schoeser, Mary, and Celia Rufey, *English and American Textiles*, 1989
Thornton, Peter, *Authentic Decor: The Domestic Interior 1620–1920*, 1984
Wells-Cole, Anthony, *Historic Paper Hangings*, Leeds City Art Galleries, 1983

Chapter Six
FURNITURE

(a) Contemporary sources

Hope, Thomas, *Household Furniture and Interior Decoration*, 1807; reprinted with an introduction by David Watkin, New York, 1971
Loudon, J. C., *An Encyclopaedia of Cottage, Farm and Villa Architecture*, 1833
Pugin, A. C., *Gothic Furniture*, 1827
Sheraton, Thomas, *The Cabinet-Maker and Upholsterer's Drawing Book*, 1791–3
——, *The Cabinet Dictionary*, 1803; reprinted, W. P. Cole and C. F. Montgomery, eds.. New York, 1970
——, *Encyclopaedia*, 1804–8
Smith, George, *A Collection of Designs for Household Furniture and Interior Decoration*, 1808; reprinted, C. F. Montgomery and B. M. Forman, eds., New York 1970
——, *The Cabinet-Maker and Upholsterer's Guide*, 1826
Tatham, C. H., *Etchings of Ancient Ornamental Architecture*, 1799–1800
Whittaker, H., *Designs of Cabinet and Upholstery Furniture*, 1825

(b) Modern sources

Agius, Pauline, ed., *Ackerman's Regency Furniture and Interiors*, 1984
Collard, Frances, *Regency Furniture*, 1985
Fastnedge, Ralph, *Sheraton Furniture*, 1962
Jourdain, Margaret, *Regency Furniture*, 1965
Walton, Karin, *The Golden Age of English Furniture Upholstery*, Leeds City Art Galleries, 1973

Chapter Seven
GARDENS

(a) Contemporary sources

Loudon, J. C., *An Encyclopaedia of Gardening*, 1822
——, *The Green-House Companion*, 1824
——, *The Suburban Gardener and Villa Companion*, 1838
——, *The Landscape Gardening . . . of Humphry Repton*, 1840
Papworth, J. B., *Hints on Ornamental Gardening*, 1823
Repton, Humphry, *Observations*, 1803

(b) Modern sources

Jacques, David, *The Georgian Garden*, 1983
Longstaffe-Gowan, Todd, *The London Town Garden*, 1992
Simo, Melanie, *Loudon and the Landscape*, 1988
Stuart, David, and James Sutherland, *Plants from the Past*, 1987

FURTHER READING OF PARTICULAR
IMPORTANCE FOR THE UNITED STATES

Andrews, Wayne, *Architecture, Ambition and Americans*, New York: Free Press, 1979

Aronson, Joseph, *The Encyclopedia of Furniture*, New York: Crown Publishers, 1965

Bjerkoe, Ethel Hall, *The Cabinetmakers of America*, Rev. ed. Exton, Pa.: Schiffer Publishing Ltd., 1978

Cornelius, Charles O., *Furniture Masterpieces of Duncan Phyfe*, 1922 (reprint, New York: Dover Publications, 1970)

Fairbanks, Jonathan L., and Bates, Elizabeth Bidwell, *American Furniture: 1620 to the Present*, New York: Richard Marek, 1981

Favretti, Rudy J., and Favretti, Joy Putnam, *Landscapes and Gardens for Historic Buildings: A Handbook for Reproducing and Recreating Authentic Landscape Settings*, Nashville, Tenn.: American Association for State and Local History, 1978

Garrett, Wendell D., and others, *The Arts in America: The Nineteenth Century*, New York: Charles Scribner's Sons, 1969

Gowans, Alan, *Images of American Living: Four Centuries of Architecture and Furniture as Cultural Expression*, 1964 (reprint, New York: Harper and Row, 1976)

Hitchcock, Henry-Russell, *Architecture: Nineteenth and Twentieth Centuries*, 1963 (reprint, Baltimore: Penguin Books, 1971)

Kennedy, Roger G., *Architecture, Men, Women and Money in America, 1600–1860*, New York: Random House, 1985

Ketchum, William C., Jr., *The Smithsonian Illustrated Library of Antiques: Furniture 2: Neoclassic to the Present*, New York: Cooper-Hewitt Museum, 1981

Kitchen, Judith L., *Caring for Your Old House: A Guide for Owners and Residents*, Washington, DC: The Preservation Press, 1991

Lynn, Catherine, Wallpaper in America, New York: W. W. Norton and Co., 1980

McAlester, Virginia, and McAlester, Lee, *A Field Guide to American Houses*, New York: Alfred Knopf, 1984

McClelland, Nancy, *Duncan Phyfe and the English Regency, 1795–1830*, 1939 (reprint, New York: Dover Publications, 1980)

Metropolitan Museum of Art, *Nineteenth-Century America: Furniture and Other Decorative Arts*, New York: New York Graphic Society, 1971.

Montgomery, Florence N., *Textiles in America, 1650–1920*, New York: W. W. Norton and Co., 1984

Moss, Roger W., *Lighting for Historic Buildings*, Washington, DC: The Preservation Press, 1988

National Trust for Historic Preservation, *Landmark Yellow Pages: Where to Find All the Names, Addresses, Facts and Figures You Need*, Washington, DC: The Preservation Press, 1992

Newark Museum, *Classical America, 1815–1845*, Newark, NJ: Newark Museum Association, 1963

Nylander, Jane C., *Fabrics for Historic Buildings*, Rev. ed. Washington, DC: The Preservation Press, 1990

Nylander, Richard C., *Wallpapers for Historic Buildings*, Rev. ed. Washington, DC: The Preservation Press, 1992

Thornton, Peter, *Authentic Decor: The Domestic Interior 1620–1920*, New York: Viking, 1984

Von Rosentiel, Helene, *American Rugs and Carpets*, New York: William Morrow and Co., 1978

Von Rosenstiel, Helene and Winkler, Gail Caskey, *Floor Coverings for Historic Buildings*, Washington, DC: The Preservation Press, 1988

ACKNOWLEDGEMENTS

Bridgeman Art Library, London, 153
Bridgeman/Private Collection 2, 3
Bridgeman/Guildhall Library, City of London 29, 63, 108, 168
Bridgeman/Victoria & Albert Museum 106, 207
Bridgeman/Christopher Wood Gallery, London 156 (main pic)
Bridgeman/City of Bristol Museum and Art Gallery 209
The British Architectural Library, RIBA, London 6, 17, 20, 28, 30, 32, 63, 76, 80, 130 (JB Archive), 133, 160, 164, 177, 180, 186, 187, 190, 196, 211, 220, 221, 223
Courtesy of *Traditional Homes* Magazine/Ian Parry 8, 142, 149
Anthony Kersting 10, 15, 31, 34, 36, 47, 206
David Enders Tripp, Homewood, The Johns Hopkins University 13, 67, 87, 97, 139, 158
National Portrait Gallery, London 14, 16, 170
John Bethell Photography 23, 41, 43, 44, 217 (below)
E. T. Archive, London 26
Lizambard Images 61
Peter Aprahamian 27, 45, 57 (above), 64, 65 (top right), 72, 78, 79, 97, 114, 117, 124, 129, 134, 135, 136, 148 (below), 150, 155, 183, 185, 204/5
Edifice, London 35, 57 (centre right), 58, 59, 65 (top left), 202
Guildhall Library, City of London (JB Archive) 39
Sotheby's, London (JB Archive) 45, 83, 104, 107, 131, 152, 218
Sir John Soane's Museum, London (JB Archive) 89
Victoria & Albert Museum, London (JB Archive) 95 (above), 157
British Museum, Banks Collection (JB Archive) 120
JB Archive 121, 127
Robert Llewellyn, Charlottesville, Virginia, 55, 57 (centre left and right), 68, 81, 134, 210
Phaidon Press 77, 85 (below right), 96
Courtesy of the Governor and Company of the Bank of England 86
Tim Mowl, Bristol 92, 101
Lambeth Archives Department, London 99, 216
National Trust Photographic Library 103, 111 (below), 200
The Mansell Collection Limited, London 109, 112, 123, 176, 189, 197
Christie's Colour Library, London 110, 111, 116, 175, 185, 189, 195, 211
Elizabeth Whiting & Associates Photo Library, London 118
Patrick Baty, Papers and Paints Ltd, London 138
Courtesy of the American Museum in Bath 145, 154, 162
Hamilton Weston Wallpapers Ltd, Richmond, Surrey 146, 147, 148
Edward Distelkamp 217

Page numbers in *italics* refer to illustrations or their captions

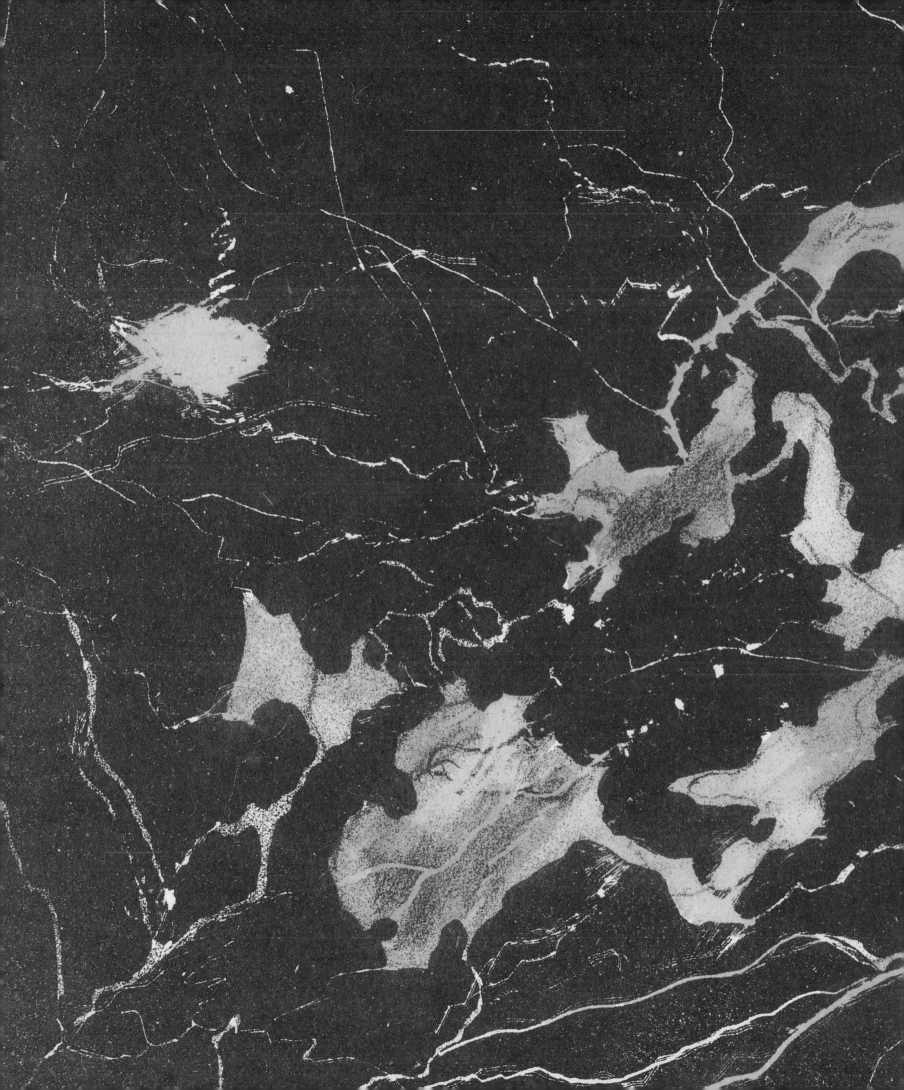